Shared Equipment Management for High-Mix, Low-Volume Manufacturing

A Practical Guide to Taming Monuments, Protecting Flow, and Unlocking Hidden Capacity

The Lean Line Pro Deep Dive Series, Vol. 7

Nick Arkesteyn

Shared Equipment Management for High-Mix, Low-Volume Manufacturing

Nick Arkesteyn

First Edition

Published by Arkesteyn Publishing

United States

ISBN 978-1-971417-06-6 (Paperback)

ISBN 978-1-971417-07-3 (eBook)

To Jesus Christ — all glory to You alone.

"...whatever you do, do all to the glory of God."

— 1 Corinthians 10:31

"Trust in the Lord with all your heart, and don't lean on your own understanding."

— Proverbs 3:5

Table of Contents

Key Terms Used in This Book

This glossary defines terms as they're used in this book. Some of these words mean different things in different contexts—especially if you've studied traditional lean manufacturing. These definitions apply specifically to high-mix, low-volume (HMLV) environments.

Andon: A visual or audible signal that communicates a problem requiring immediate attention. In this book, an Andon event is triggered when the Input Buffer drops below the Red Line.

Buffer: A controlled amount of inventory placed before or after the monument to absorb variability. Not to be confused with uncontrolled WIP piling up on the floor. A buffer has a defined size, a Green/Yellow/Red zone, and a MAX Line.

Buffer Health: A Monument Scorecard metric tracking the percentage of time the Input Buffer stays in the Green Zone. Target: >80% Green.

Campaign Wheel: A fixed, repeating sequence of product families through the constraint, designed to minimize total changeover time by running similar setups back-to-back. The wheel turns on a set cycle (daily, every 2–3 days, or weekly).

Communication Burst: A rapid, scripted notification sequence triggered when the monument goes down. The goal is to inform Maintenance, the Supervisor, and the Water Strider within 5 minutes so that no one wastes time wondering what happened.

CONWIP (Constant Work-In-Process): A system that limits total WIP at the constraint using physical Tickets. Work cannot be released to the monument without a Ticket, and Tickets only become available when finished work exits the system. Also referred to as the Ticket System in this book.

Constraint: The single shared resource you are focused on improving. In this book, the constraint is the monument that limits overall plant throughput. We address one constraint at a time.

Constraint Lead Time: The total elapsed time from when a batch leaves the cell (Cell OUT) to when it returns (Cell IN) after processing through the monument. Target: less than 2x the actual process time.

Effective Utilization: The percentage of time the monument is producing good parts on scheduled work. Excludes running ahead of schedule, reworking defects, and running unauthorized jobs. Not the same as "machine running."

Expedite Rate: The percentage of jobs flowing through the monument that carry a Priority Tag (Red or Yellow). Used as a diagnostic for system health. Target: below 20%.

FIFO (First In, First Out): A sequencing rule where jobs are processed in the order they arrive. Enforced physically with a lane or rack that prevents cherry-picking. In this book, FIFO is often combined with a Priority Tag system for genuine emergencies.

Flex Slot: A reserved time block at the end of a Campaign Wheel rotation dedicated to running Strangers (non-standard jobs). Fixed in timing, variable in content. Should not exceed 15% of total wheel time.

Gatekeeper: The person (typically the Water Strider) who inspects every batch against the Release Checklist before it enters the monument's queue / Input Buffer. Has absolute authority to reject incomplete work.

Gatekeeper Checklist: A printed checklist used at every handoff to verify that work is complete, documented, and ready to run. If any box is unchecked, the batch stays in the cell.

Green Zone / Yellow Zone / Red Zone: Visual management zones painted on or near the buffer to indicate health status. Green means healthy, Yellow means watch, Red means escalate immediately.

Handoff: The transfer of ownership of a batch from one person or area to another (Cell to Water Strider, Water Strider to Monument, Monument to Cell). Each handoff has a defined location, a checklist, and a signature requirement.

Handoff Card: A physical card attached to each batch that documents the chain of custody—who released it, who received it, and who returned it. Tracks priority, recipe, quantity, and total lead time.

Heartbeat: The rhythm of the constraint. Calculated as Average Process Cycle + Average Changeover. Sets the pace for the Water Strider route, cell batch sizes, and plant-wide synchronization.

Input Buffer: Inventory staged before the monument to prevent starvation. Sized based on upstream replenishment time multiplied by a variability factor. Contains a Warning Line at 50% as a check upstream trigger and Red Line at 25% as an escalation trigger.

MAX Line: The upper limit of the Output Buffer. When the buffer reaches the MAX Line, the monument must stop producing—even if it could keep running. Prevents overproduction.

Monument: Any machine, process, or resource that multiple production cells must share because it is too expensive to duplicate, too large to fit in a cell, or requires scarce specialized skills. Examples: heat treat oven, centralized paint booth, large CNC machining center.

Monument Scorecard: A weekly tracking tool for the six key metrics: Effective Utilization, Changeover Trend, Buffer Health, Constraint Lead Time, Expedite Rate, and Customer Service Level. Reviewed every Monday.

No-Fly Zone: A marked area (typically a red line) around the monument. Only the Monument Operator and Water Strider may enter. Prevents cell operators from hovering, interrupting, or attempting to jump the queue.

Output Buffer: Inventory staged after the monument to protect downstream cells from monument stoppages. Sized based on the monument's 80th-percentile repair time multiplied by downstream consumption rate.

Phantom Backlog: Work released to the monument's queue / Input Buffer that is not actually ready to run—missing parts, incomplete paperwork, wrong containers. Creates the illusion of a full queue while the monument sits idle waiting for something it can actually process.

Priority Tag: A visual indicator (Red or Yellow) attached to a job that allows it to bypass standard FIFO sequencing. Red = Emergency (line down, safety). Yellow = Late. Must be capped at less than 20% of total jobs.

Red Line: A physical mark on the Input Buffer (wall, rack, or floor) indicating the minimum acceptable inventory level—typically set at 25% of the buffer. When inventory drops below the Red Line, the Water Strider escalates immediately.

Release Rules: The set of conditions that must be met before work is allowed to enter the monument queue. Enforced by the Gatekeeper Checklist. The foundational discipline that must be in place before any scheduling strategy will work.

Runners: High-volume, frequently repeating product families. Typically the top 20% of SKUs by volume. Candidates for Supermarket buffering.

SMED (Single-Minute Exchange of Die): A methodology for reducing changeover time. In HMLV, the goal is not necessarily sub-10-minute setups but reducing changeover enough to cut batch sizes in half. Covered in detail in Book 2 of this series.

Strangers: Low-volume, infrequent, or one-off jobs that do not fit neatly into any standard product family. Handled through the Flex Slot on a Campaign Wheel or processed via FIFO in a general queue.

Supermarket: A controlled inventory buffer of pre-built standard parts (Runners) that downstream cells pull from as needed. Decouples the cells from the monument for repetitive work. Not suitable for custom or one-off jobs.

Ticket (WIP Ticket): A physical token (laminated card or magnetic marker) that authorizes a cell to release one batch to the monument. The total number of Tickets in circulation equals the WIP cap. No Ticket = No Release.

Time-Slicing: A scheduling strategy that divides monument availability into fixed time windows assigned to specific cells. Each cell gets guaranteed access during their window. Use It or Lose It—if a cell is not ready during their window, the time goes to the next cell.

Value Time: The portion of monument running time spent producing good parts on sold, scheduled orders. Distinct from Loss Time (changeovers, breakdowns) and Waste Time (running ahead, rework, unauthorized jobs).

Variability Factor: A multiplier used in buffer sizing to account for upstream unreliability. Ranges from 1.5x (stable) to 3.0x (unstable). Applied to the replenishment time to calculate Input Buffer size.

Warning Line: A physical mark on the Input Buffer (wall, rack, or floor)—typically set at 50% of the buffer. When inventory drops below the Warning Line, the Water Strider checks upstream for delays.

Water Strider: A dedicated material handler who runs a fixed route between cells and the monument at a frequency of every half-heartbeat. Responsible for feeding the monument, guarding the gate (rejecting incomplete work), and returning finished parts to cells. The single point of accountability for material flow through the constraint.

Waste Time: Monument running time that produces no value—running ahead of schedule, reworking defective parts, or processing large batches solely to avoid changeovers. The machine is busy, but the business gains nothing.

Introduction

The Elephant in the Room

If you are reading this book, you probably have a machine in your factory that everyone hates.

It might be a heat treat oven. It might be a massive paint booth, a plating line, or a million-dollar CNC machining center. Whatever it is, it has three characteristics:

1. **It is expensive.** (You can't afford to buy five of them.)
2. **It is huge.** (You can't fit it inside a work cell.)
3. **Multiple cells have to share it.** (Maybe two cells. Maybe every cell in the plant. Either way, they take turns, they fight for

access, and they blame each other when things go wrong.)

In Lean manufacturing, we call this a "Monument." It stands in the middle of your factory like a statue in a park, forcing all traffic to go around it.

For decades, traditional Lean consultants have given High-Mix, Low-Volume (HMLV) manufacturers the same advice regarding monuments: *"Eliminate them. Break them up. Buy small, dedicated equipment for every cell."*

That advice is beautiful. It is also expensive, impractical, and often impossible.

When you are running 18,000 SKUs through a single facility, you cannot buy 18,000 dedicated machines. When your heat treat oven requires a certified metallurgist to operate, you cannot clone that person for every cell.

So, you are stuck. You have cells that flow perfectly inside themselves... right up until they need to use that shared machine. Then they fight. Maybe it is just two cells sharing a CNC and arguing daily over who runs first. Maybe it is seven cells plus engineering runs plus one-offs plus low runners plus the zombie parts nobody wants to kill, all funneling through one oven at the back of the plant. The scale changes. The problem does not.

Flow dies. Work piles up. Lead times explode. Schedulers start screaming. Your "Lean" factory turns into a parking lot.

This book is the solution to that problem.

The New Rule: Manage, Don't Eliminate

This is **Volume 7** of the *Lean Line Pro Deep Dive Series*. In the previous books, we taught you how to group product families (Book 1), slash changeover times (Book 2), design flexible cells (Book 3), level your schedule (Book 4), install pull systems (Book 5), and arrange your whole facility for flow (Book 6). Those six books get you to a running HMLV operation. This book handles what happens when two cells, or ten cells, or every cell in the plant, has to flow through the same machine.

Now, we tackle the reality of the shared resource.

We are not going to tell you to buy five new ovens. We are not going to tell you to redesign your entire factory to eliminate the monument. Instead, we are going to teach you how to manage the constraint so effectively that it stops dominating the plant.

We will accept the reality of the shared resource and build a nervous system around it. This system is made from buffers, signals, and rules that prevent starvation and flooding.

How to Use This Book

This is not a textbook. It is an implementation guide.

We have stripped out the theory. We have removed the academic fluff. If you have read Books 1–6, you already know the basics of Lean. We won't bore you by reteaching them here.

This book is divided into two parts:

Part 1: The Strategy (Chapters 1–7) Here we cover the decision-making framework. You will learn:

- How to diagnose if your problem is scheduling, capacity, or reliability.
- The six strategies for managing shared equipment (from Time-Slicing to Campaign Wheels).

- How to design cells that "hand off" work to a monument without losing ownership.
- The "Heartbeat" concept that synchronizes your entire plant to the constraint.

Part 2: The Toolkit (Appendices) This is your "copy/paste" resource. It contains the exact templates, checklists, and scorecards you need to run the system.

- **The Monument Scorecard:** To track the six metrics that matter.
- **The Gatekeeper Checklist:** To stop bad work from entering the monument's queue / input buffer.
- **The Handoff Card:** To maintain chain-of-custody between cells.
- **The ROI Calculator:** To prove the value of your improvements to Finance.

Is This the Right Book for You?

Before we go further, make sure you are in the right place.

This book is about **shared equipment.** Two or more cells have to use the same machine. The fight is over access. Who gets the machine when. How you schedule it. How you keep the sharing from turning into daily expedite meetings.

This works at any scale. It works when two cells share a CNC. It works when three cells share a plating line. It works when every cell in the plant funnels through one oven. The strategies in this book scale with the problem.

But if your problem is different, you may need a different book. If you have ONE cell, and ONE station inside that cell is a batch processor that physically needs 10 or 20 or 80 parts at a time, you have a flow problem inside that cell, not an access problem across cells. That station is breaking your single-piece flow. **Volume 8, *Batch Processor Management for High-Mix, Low-Volume Manufacturing*, covers that situation.**

The equipment does not decide which book you need. Who uses the machine decides.

- One machine, two or more cells sharing it = this book
- One machine inside one cell, running batches = Volume 8

- Both situations in the same plant = read this one first, then Volume 8

Chapter 2 of this book has a diagnostic that will help you confirm which problem you actually have.

The Promise

If you follow the rules in this book, you will not fix the monument. The monument is a machine; it doesn't care about your problems.

But you *will* fix the chaos around it.

You will stop the daily expedite meetings. You will stop the finger-pointing between cell supervisors. You will replace "heroic effort" with boring, predictable, profitable consistency.

Your constraint is waiting. Let’s get to work.

Nick Arkesteyn *Manufacturing Engineer & Founder, Lean Line Pro*

Part 1

Operating System

Chapter 1

The Shared Equipment Reality

Shared equipment is the reality of High-Mix, Low-Volume (HMLV) manufacturing. You make 50 different hydraulic valves, not one million identical widgets. You have 200 SKUs, not three. You cannot afford to buy a dedicated heat treat oven for every product family, nor do you have the floor space for them.

Shared equipment (often called a "Monument") is any machine, process, or resource that multiple production cells or value streams must use to complete their products.

It usually exists because of three constraints:

1. **Cost:** The machine is too expensive to duplicate (e.g., a $500k CNC center).
2. **Space:** The machine is physically too large to fit in a cell (e.g., a centralized paint booth).
3. **Specialization:** The process requires scarce skills (e.g., a certified heat treat technician).

Traditional Lean advice says, "Eliminate shared resources. Create dedicated cells." In HMLV, that advice usually isn't practical. You cannot buy your way out of this problem. You must manage your way out.

The Three Problems Shared Equipment Creates

When unmanaged, shared equipment creates a chain reaction that destroys flow.

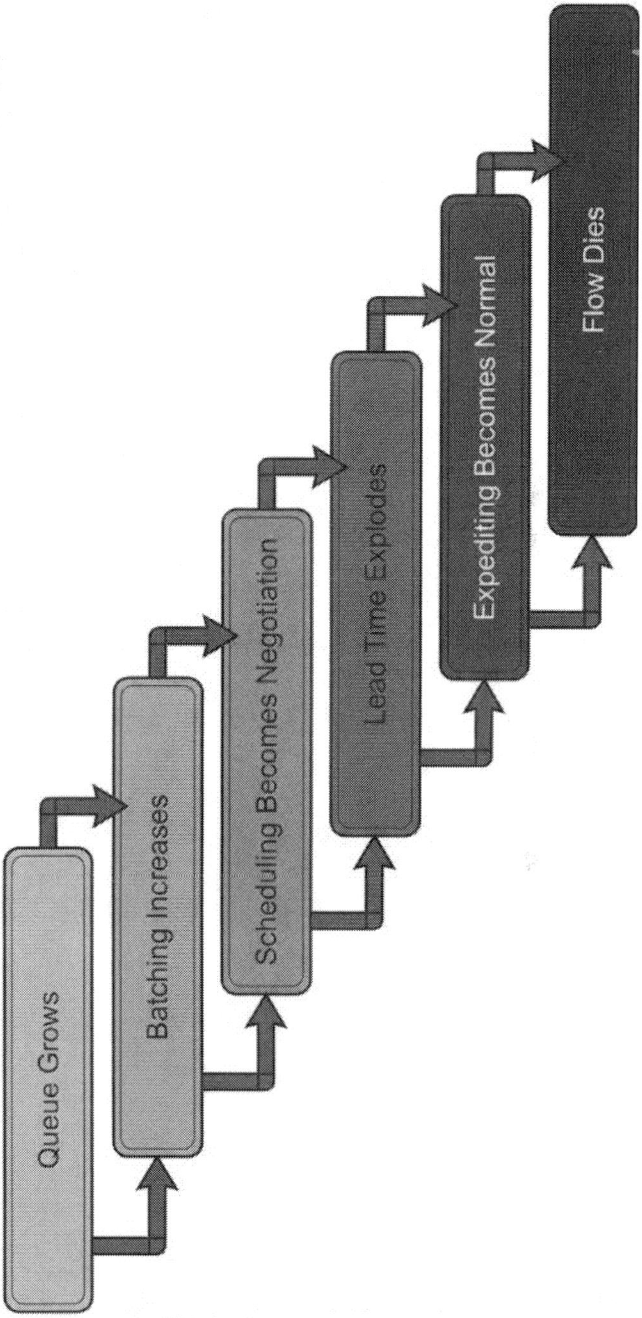
Queue Grows
Batching Increases
Scheduling Becomes Negotiation
Lead Time Explodes
Expediting Becomes Normal
Flow Dies

The Chain Reaction:

1. **Queue Grows:** Work piles up waiting for access.
2. **Batching Increases:** Operators run larger batches to "maximize efficiency" and minimize changeovers.
3. **Scheduling Becomes Negotiation:** Cell leads fight for machine time.
4. **Lead Time Explodes:** Days become weeks.
5. **Expediting Becomes Normal:** Everything is "hot," so nothing is.
6. **Flow Dies:** The chaos ripples back upstream to every cell.

Every strategy in this book is aimed at stopping this chain at Step 1 and Step 2: uncontrolled release and batching.

The 20% Expedite Rule

This is your primary diagnostic for system health.

If more than 20% of jobs going through your shared equipment are "priority" or "expedited," you do not have a scheduling system—you have negotiation.

- **< 20% Expedited:** System is working. Exceptions are manageable.
- **20-35% Expedited:** System is stressed. Flow is compromised.
- **> 35% Expedited:** System is broken. Standard lead times are meaningless.

This is not a finance-grade KPI cutoff. It is an operating-system alarm bell. Once expedites become routine, scheduling has collapsed into negotiation.

The Fundamental Tension: Utilization vs. Flow

At the core of every shared equipment decision is a conflict between two legitimate business goals: **Maximizing Utilization** and **Maximizing Flow**. You cannot maximize both simultaneously.

Goal	**Utilization Focus (Traditional)**	**Flow Focus (Lean)**
Batch Size	Large (Keep machine busy)	Small (Keep parts moving)
Changeovers	Few (avoid downtime)	Frequent (enable mix)
WIP Inventory	High	Low
Response Time	Slow (weeks)	Fast (days)
Mindset	"Make the machine efficient"	"Make the customer happy"

The Solution: For shared equipment in HMLV, a practical starting point is **65–80% effective utilization**, not 95% machine running time. You must accept that 20–35% of capacity will be "lost" to changeovers and buffers. You are trading that theoretical capacity for actual cash flow and speed.

Effective Utilization: Value vs. Waste

A machine running at 90% utilization is losing money if it is running the wrong parts. We distinguish between three types of time:

1. **Value Time:** Running the right jobs at the right time (sold orders).
2. **Loss Time:** Equipment unavailable (changeovers, breakdowns, maintenance).
3. **Waste Time:** Equipment running, but adding no value (running ahead of schedule, reworking parts, or running large batches to avoid changeovers).

The goal of this book is to maximize **Value Time**, not just running time.

The "Never Depend on Heroes" Principle

If your shared equipment requires a "hero" to run like a master scheduler who keeps it all in their head, or a wizard operator who is the only one who can change it over, you do not have an efficient system. Heroes burn out. Heroes take vacations.

We will replace heroics with:

- **Visual Scheduling:** That anyone can read.
- **Fixed Rules:** That anyone can follow.
- **Standard Work:** That allows any trained operator to run the equipment effectively.

The Strategy: One Shared Resource at a Time

Do not try to fix every monument in your plant simultaneously. Pick one. Fix one. Prove the system works.

The Roadmap:

- **Part 1 (The Strategy):** We will assess your constraint, select a management strategy (Time-Slicing, FIFO, or Campaign Wheels), and redesign the material flow.

- **Part 2 (The Toolkit):** We will provide the checklists, scorecards, and standard work templates to sustain the change.

Chapter 2

Selecting and Assessing Your Constraint

You likely have multiple shared resources: the oven, the wash station, the CMM, the insert press. To succeed, you must focus your resources on the one that is hurting your business the most.

Selection Criteria

Rate your shared resources on these five factors (1–5 scale):

1. **Pain Level:** Where is the most firefighting and overtime occurring?

2. **Lead Time Impact:** Where do parts sit the longest?

3. **Flow Impact:** Which resource disrupts the most downstream cells?

4. **Improvement Potential:** Is the team willing? Is the equipment capable?

5. **Learning Value:** Will solving this teach you skills applicable elsewhere?

*See **Appendix A** for the complete **Selection Matrix Template**.*

The Constraint Type Test

Before you spend money on new equipment, you must diagnose *why* the resource is a bottleneck. Most "capacity" problems are actually scheduling problems.

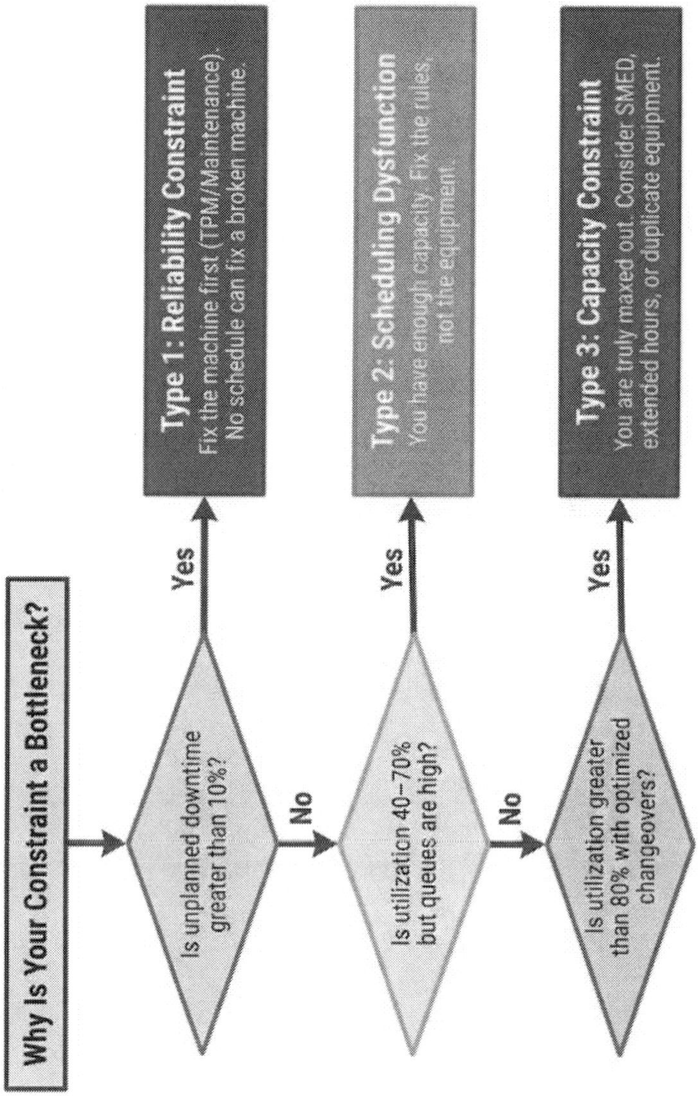
Why Is Your Constraint a Bottleneck?
Is unplanned downtime greater than 10%?
Yes
Type 1: Reliability Constraint
Fix the machine first (TPM/Maintenance). No schedule can fix a broken machine.
No
Is utilization 40–70% but queues are high?
Yes
Type 2: Scheduling Dysfunction
You have enough capacity. Fix the rules, not the equipment.
No
Is utilization greater than 80% with optimized changeovers?
Yes
Type 3: Capacity Constraint
You are truly maxed out. Consider SMED, extended hours, or duplicate equipment.

Type 1: Reliability Constraint

- **Symptom:** Unplanned downtime > 10%.
- **Diagnosis:** The machine is broken.
- **Solution:** Fix stability (TPM/Maintenance) *before* attempting to improve flow. No schedule can fix a broken machine.

Type 2: Scheduling Dysfunction

- **Symptom:** Utilization is moderate (40–70%), yet queues are high. Hot jobs constantly jump the line. The machine sits idle waiting for "full batches."
- **Diagnosis:** You have enough capacity, but you are managing it poorly.
- **Solution:** Implement release rules, FIFO, and visual management (Chapters 3 & 5). **Do not buy more equipment.**

Type 3: Capacity Constraint

- **Symptom:** Equipment runs > 80% utilization reliably. Changeovers are optimized. The queue exists simply because demand exceeds supply.

- **Diagnosis:** You are truly maxed out.
- **Solution:** Aggressive SMED (Book 2), extended hours, or buying duplicate equipment (Strategy 6 in Chapter 3).

Measuring What Matters

Gut feel is not data. To fix the constraint, you need a baseline. Capture these five metrics for one week:

1. Utilization Breakdown: Don't just track "running." Track:

- **Running:** (Processing parts)
- **Changeover:** (Setup/Teardown)
- **Waiting:** (Idle/No Operator/No Parts)
- **Down:** (Broken)

2. Changeover Time

Measure from the last good part of Product A to the first good part of Product B. Reference Book 2 (SMED) for the detailed measurement protocol. Note the *variability*. If one operator takes 45 minutes and another takes 2 hours, you have a standardization problem.

3. Queue Time (The Snapshot Technique)

You don't need complex software. Walk to the constraint at the same time every day for 5 days. Count the number of carts/totes waiting. Note the date on the oldest traveler.

- *Queue < 1 Shift:* Healthy.
- *Queue 1–3 Days:* Stressed (Batching or Capacity issue).
- *Queue > 3 Days:* Crisis (Scheduling dysfunction).

4. Demand Variability (The Napkin Test)

Look at the last 10 weeks of demand. Is the busiest week more than **2x** the volume of the slowest week?

- **Yes:** High variability. You need flexible scheduling (FIFO/Supermarkets).
- **No:** Stable. You can use fixed scheduling (Time-Slicing/Campaign Wheels).

5. Setup Frequency

How often do you change over? If you change over 5 times a week and lose 2 hours each time, you are losing 10 hours (one full shift) to setups. This is your "hidden" capacity factory.

Calculating the Cost of the Constraint

To get leadership support, you must translate these problems into dollars.

The Cost Iceberg:

- **Visible Costs:** Overtime, Expediting Fees, Premium Freight.
- **Hidden Costs (The "Killer" Costs):**
  - **Lost Sales:** Revenue lost because lead times were too long.
  - **WIP Carrying Cost:** Not just at the machine, but the "Batching Ripple" of inventory stuck in upstream cells waiting for the monument.
  - **Quality:** Rework caused by rushing.

Action: Fill out the **Cost of Constraint Worksheet** (Appendix A) and get your Finance Controller to sign off on it. A number validated by

Finance is a fact; a number calculated by Operations is an opinion.

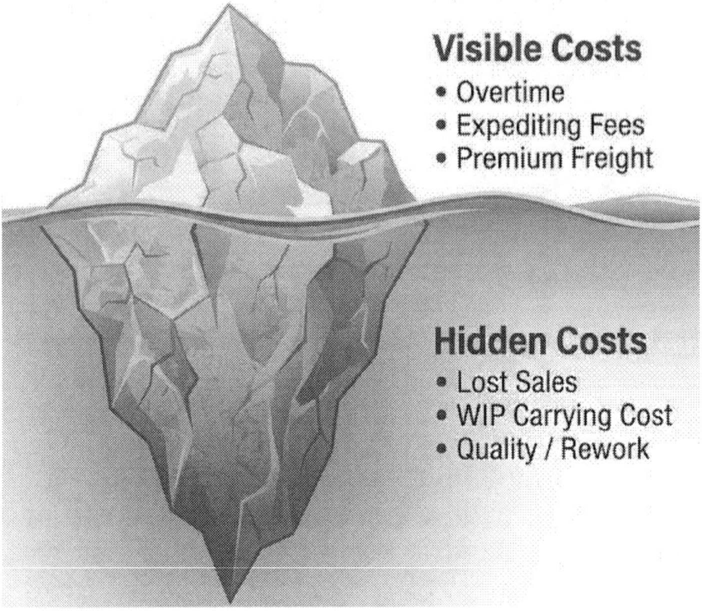

Chapter 3

The Six Management Strategies

You have assessed your constraint. You know if it is a scheduling problem, a capacity problem, or both. Now you need to choose how to fix it.

We will use six proven strategies. In practice, you will likely combine two or three of these.

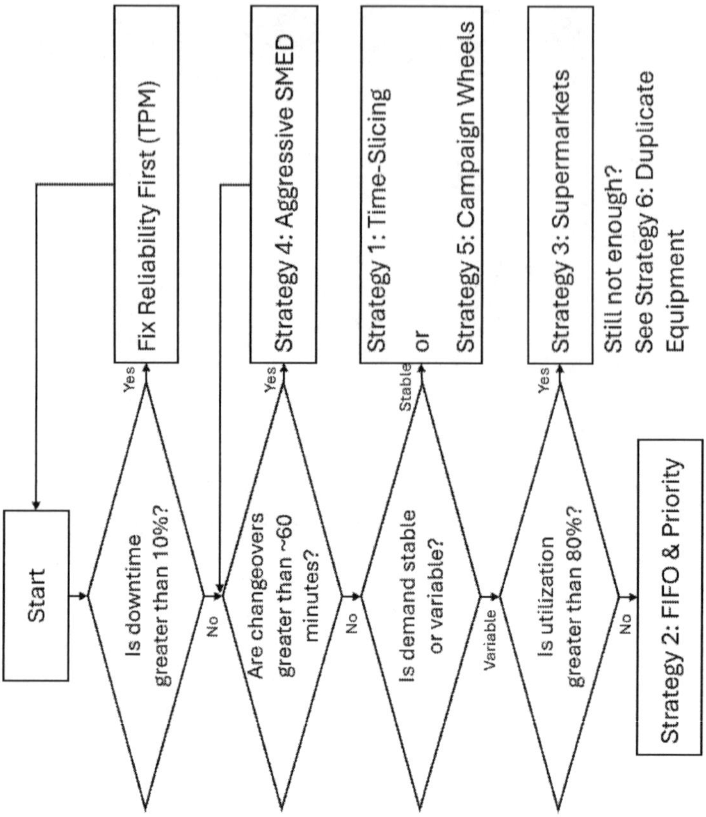

The Foundation: Release Rules

Before you implement any strategy, you must stop the bleeding. Most shared equipment chaos is not caused by the machine; it is caused by **uncontrolled job release**. Work floods into the queue without gates, creating a "phantom backlog" of jobs that are not actually ready to run.

The Gatekeeper Rule:

Only release work to the constraint queue when **ALL** of the following are true:

1. **Material is Complete:** No partial kits.
2. **Upstream is Done:** No "almost ready."
3. **Paperwork is Correct:** Recipe and specs verified.
4. **Queue Space Exists:** The lane / input buffer is not full.

*See **Appendix A** for the printable **Gatekeeper Checklist**.*

The Strategy Menu

Strategy	Best Used When...	Cost	Timeline
1. Time-Slicing	Multiple cells need predictable access. Demand is stable.	Low	Weeks

Strategy	Best Used When...	Cost	Timeline
2. FIFO + Priority	Demand is variable. Work arrives irregularly.	Low	Weeks
3. Supermarkets	Utilization is high (>80%). You need to decouple cells from the constraint.	Med	Weeks
4. Aggressive SMED	Changeovers are greater than ~60 minutes. Long setups are forcing large batches.	Med	Days

Strategy	Best Used When...	Cost	Timeline
5. Campaign Wheels	You have 5–15 product families and want to optimize sequence.	Low	Weeks
6. Duplicate Equipment	You have a true capacity constraint after exhausting Strategies 1–5.	High	Months

Strategy 1: Time-Slicing (Fixed Intervals)

Divide equipment availability into fixed time blocks. Each cell gets dedicated access during their assigned window. The full cycle of all windows is one rotation. It can repeat daily, every two days, or weekly depending on your demand and changeover times. This eliminates the daily "fight" for machine time. See the “one rotation” example below.

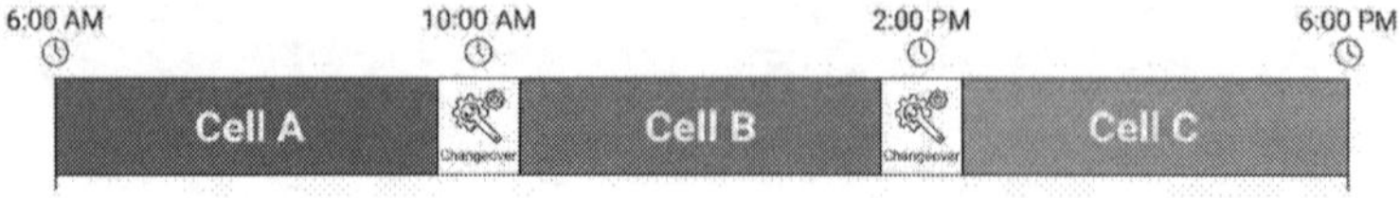

The Rules:

- **Use It or Lose It:** If Cell A isn't ready during their window, their time slot goes unused. The monument runs maintenance or waits for Cell B's scheduled window. Cell A's work waits for the next rotation. The lost time is visible and intentional. It creates the urgency to be prepared.
- **Hard Stop:** When the window ends, loading stops. Maintaining the discipline of the schedule matters more than squeezing out extra volume.
- **Visual Enforcement:** Use a countdown timer at the machine.

Best For: Moderate utilization (50–75%) where predictability is more important than raw speed.

Strategy 2: FIFO with Priority Rules

Run work in the order it arrives. This is the simplest method for high-mix environments where demand cannot be predicted.

The Physical Requirement:

You must create a **Physical FIFO Lane** with a WIP cap.

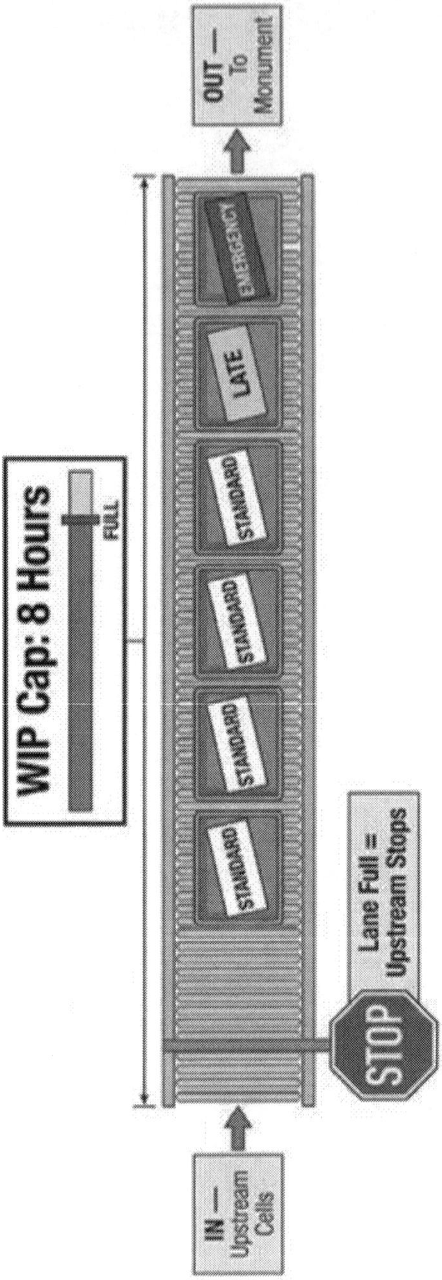
WIP Cap: 8 Hours
FULL
OUT — To Monument
EMERGENCY
LATE
STANDARD
STANDARD
STANDARD
STANDARD
Lane Full = Upstream Stops
STOP
IN — Upstream Calls

- **The Cap:** As a starting point, limit the lane to roughly one shift of work (about 8 hours in most plants). Adjust based on your actual throughput rate.

- **The Rule:** If the lane is full, upstream cells **STOP**. They do not stack parts on the floor.

Priority Discipline:

Strict FIFO fails when "hot" jobs get stuck behind low-priority work. You need a priority system, but it must be capped.

- **Red Tag:** Emergency (Line down, safety). Jumps to front.

- **Yellow Tag:** Late. Jumps ahead of standard.

- **Standard:** FIFO.

The 20% Rule: If more than 20% of your jobs have Priority Tags, you do not have a system; you have chaos. Fix your lead times.

Strategy 3: Supermarkets (The Decoupling Point)

Place inventory buffers *before* and *after* the monument to absorb variability.

- **Input Buffer:** Allows the monument to run continuously even if a cell stops.
- **Output Buffer:** Allows downstream cells to keep working even if the monument stops.

Warning: Do not use Supermarkets for custom/one-off work. A supermarket requires repetitive product families. If every job is unique, use a FIFO lane.

*Refer to **Book 5 (Material Flow)** for detailed calculations on Buffer Sizing.*

Strategy 4: Aggressive SMED

If changeovers are routinely taking 60 minutes or more, this is likely your first priority. The exact threshold depends on your process cycle. But once setups start forcing large batches to justify the time, SMED becomes urgent. You cannot flow product if you lose 2 hours every time you switch families.

The HMLV Goal:

You are not trying to get to "Single Minute" (9 minutes) just for bragging rights. You are trying to reduce changeover enough to **cut your batch sizes in half**.

- **Traditional:** 2-hour setup → Run 500 parts → Lead time: 2 weeks.
- **SMED Target:** 20-minute setup → Run 50 parts → Lead time: 2 days.

*Refer to **Book 2 (SMED)** for the step-by-step reduction protocol.*

Strategy 5: Campaign Wheels

Instead of random sequencing, run product families in a fixed, repeating sequence (The Wheel) that minimizes changeover penalties.

Most HMLV shops schedule their monuments reactively. Whatever is "hot" runs next. This means the oven might go from Family A to Family E to Family B to Family A again. This can cause a full changeover penalty every time. Where running A → B → E in a fixed sequence would have cut total setup time by 40%.

A Campaign Wheel is a predetermined rotation of product families through the constraint. Think of it like a bus schedule: each family has a "stop" on the wheel, and the wheel turns on a fixed cycle (daily, every two days, or weekly depending on your demand).

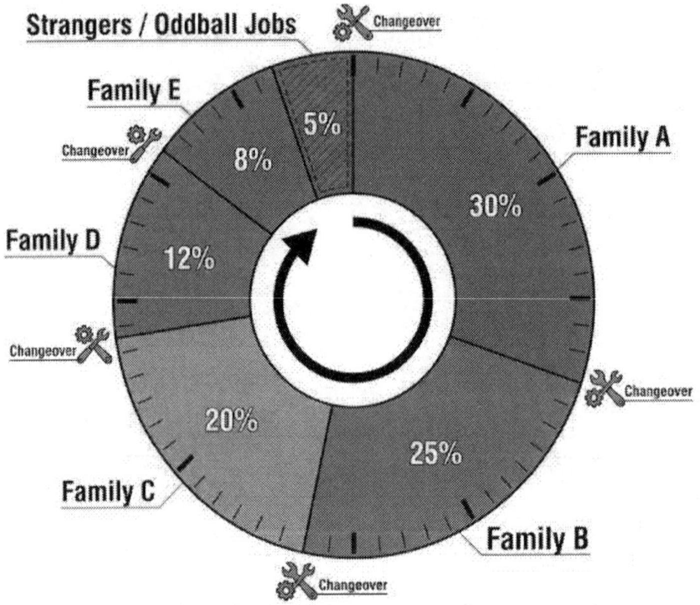

Why It Works in HMLV

Random scheduling punishes you twice:

1. You take unnecessary changeovers because you bounce between dissimilar families.
2. You lose predictability because no one knows when their family will run next.

A Campaign Wheel fixes both. You sequence families so that each changeover is the shortest possible (similar setups back-to-back), and every cell knows exactly when their work will hit the machine.

Building the Wheel: Step by Step

Step 1: List Your Families

Pull the product families that flow through the constraint. If you have completed Book 1 (Product Families), you already have this. If not, group by setup similarity—parts that share the same fixtures, temperatures, or tooling belong together.

Example: A heat treat oven serves five families.

Family	Temp Range	Fixture	Avg Weekly Demand
A - Steel Shafts	1500°F	Basket 1	40 parts
B - Steel Housings	1500°F	Basket 2	30 parts
C - Aluminum Bodies	900°F	Rack 1	25 parts
D - Aluminum Caps	900°F	Rack 1	15 parts
E - Specialty Alloys	1200°F	Custom	8 parts

Step 2: Sequence by Changeover Similarity

You want the shortest changeover between each stop on the wheel. Group families that share temperature, tooling, or fixtures next to each other.

Bad Sequence (Random):

A (1500°F) → D (900°F) → E (1200°F) → B (1500°F) → C (900°F)

Every stop requires a temperature change and likely a fixture swap. Total changeover: 5 full setups.

Good Sequence (Optimized Wheel):

A (1500°F) → B (1500°F) → E (1200°F) → C (900°F) → D (900°F)

A to B: Same temperature, swap basket only (10 min). B to E: Temperature drop, fixture change (25 min). E to C: Temperature drop, fixture change (20 min). C to D: Same temperature, same rack (5 min).

Transition	**Random Sequence**	**Optimized Wheel**
Stop 1 → 2	35 min	10 min
Stop 2 → 3	30 min	25 min
Stop 3 → 4	35 min	20 min
Stop 4 → 5	30 min	5 min
Total	**130 min**	**60 min**

That is 70 minutes of capacity recovered per wheel turn—just by changing the order.

Step 3: Size Each Window

Each family gets a time window proportional to its demand. Do not give equal time to unequal demand.

Using the example above, total weekly demand is 118 parts. If the oven runs 40 hours/week with a 90-minute heartbeat:

- Family A (40 parts, 34% of demand): Gets 13.5 hours.
- Family B (30 parts, 25%): Gets 10 hours.
- Family C (25 parts, 21%): Gets 8.5 hours.
- Family D (15 parts, 13%): Gets 5 hours.
- Family E (8 parts, 7%): Gets 3 hours.

Round to the nearest half-shift for simplicity. Precision is the enemy of adoption. If operators need a calculator to figure out the schedule, they will ignore it.

Step 4: Set the Cycle Time (How Often the Wheel Turns)

This is the critical decision. How long is one full rotation?

- **Daily Wheel:** The entire sequence runs every day. Best for high-demand constraints with short changeovers (<15 min). Gives maximum responsiveness.
- **2–3 Day Wheel:** Most common for HMLV. Each family runs once every 2–3 days. Balances responsiveness with changeover cost.
- **Weekly Wheel:** Each family runs once per week. Use only when changeovers are still long (>45 min) or demand is very low.

The Guideline: Your wheel cycle should be as short as your changeover times allow. If SMED has gotten you to 15-minute setups, you can afford a daily wheel. If setups are still 45 minutes, a weekly wheel prevents you from losing an entire shift to changeovers.

The Flex Slot: Handling Strangers

In HMLV, you will almost always have "Strangers." The oddball orders that do not fit any family on the wheel. A prototype. A rush order for a discontinued product. A one-time custom job.

Do not let Strangers hijack the wheel. Reserve a dedicated time block at the end of the rotation.

The Flex Slot Rules:

- **Fixed Time, Variable Content:** Friday afternoon (or the last 4 hours of your wheel) is reserved for Strangers. What runs in that slot changes; when it runs does not.
- **No Bumping:** A Stranger never bumps a standard family off the wheel. If the Flex Slot is full, the Stranger waits for the next rotation.
- **Cap It:** As a rule of thumb, keep the Flex Slot around 10–15% of total wheel time. If Strangers routinely exceed 15%, you have a product family problem—go back to Book 1.

Adjusting the Wheel: When Demand Shifts

A Campaign Wheel is not set in stone. Review and adjust monthly using this protocol:

1. Pull the last 4 weeks of demand by family.
2. Compare actual demand to the wheel allocation.

3. If a family consistently uses less than 70% of its window, shrink it.

4. If a family consistently overflows its window, expand it—but only by taking time from an underutilized family.

5. Never add time to the wheel. The total must stay fixed. If everything is overflowing, the problem is capacity, not scheduling.

The Visual: Making the Wheel Visible

Post a large, physical wheel on the wall next to the monument. Use a clock-face format or a simple color-coded weekly grid. Every cell lead should be able to glance at it and answer two questions:

1. "When does my family run next?"

2. "How many hours do I have?"

If they cannot answer both questions in under 5 seconds, your visual is too complicated. Simplify it.

Common Mistakes

1. **Equal Time for Unequal Demand.** Giving every family the same window because "it's fair" guarantees that high-

demand families starve and low-demand families waste capacity.

2. **Too Many Families on the Wheel.** If you have more than 8–10 families, the wheel becomes unwieldy. Combine low-volume families into a single "Misc" slot or use the Flex Slot.

3. **Ignoring Sequence.** Building the wheel without optimizing the changeover sequence defeats the purpose. The order matters as much as the allocation.

4. **No Flex Slot.** Pretending every job fits a family is fantasy in HMLV. Without the Flex Slot, Strangers will break the wheel within a week.

Strategy 6: Duplicate Equipment (The Nuclear Option)

Sometimes, you just need another machine. But you must **"Earn the Right to Buy."**

Before you sign a PO for $250,000, you must prove:

1. Reliability is stable (downtime <10%).

2. Scheduling is disciplined (not just chaos).

3. Changeovers are optimized (SMED applied).

If you have done 1–3 and you are *still* out of capacity, buy the machine. If not, you are just buying a second problem.

*See **Appendix A** for the **Duplicate Equipment ROI Calculator**.*

Combining Strategies: The Real-World Playbook

In the previous sections, we presented six strategies as if they were independent choices. On paper, they are. On the factory floor, they never work alone.

Every successful shared equipment system we have seen uses two or three strategies in combination. The question is not "which strategy should I pick?" It is "which combination fits my situation?"

Why Single Strategies Fail

Each strategy solves one problem well but leaves gaps.

- Time-Slicing gives you predictability, but it cannot handle demand spikes. If Cell A has a surge week and Cell B has nothing, the fixed windows waste capacity.

- FIFO gives you flexibility, but without release rules and WIP caps, it degenerates into a free-for-all within days.
- Supermarkets decouple your cells from the constraint, but they require inventory investment and only work for repetitive families.
- SMED reduces changeover time, but faster setups alone do not tell you what to run next or how much WIP to allow in the queue.
- Campaign Wheels optimize your sequence, but they assume relatively stable demand. A wheel cannot react to a Monday morning emergency.

No single strategy covers scheduling, sequencing, WIP control, and variability absorption simultaneously. You need a combination.

The Three Proven Combinations

The most successful implementations fall into one of three patterns. Find the one that matches your situation.

Combination 1: Campaign Wheel + FIFO Flex Slot + SMED

Best For: Moderate utilization (50–75%). Mix of repeatable families and occasional strangers. Changeovers are currently long but reducible.

How It Works:

- The Campaign Wheel sets the weekly sequence for your top product families. Each family knows when it runs and for how long.
- The Flex Slot at the end of the wheel handles strangers and one-off jobs using FIFO rules. Whatever arrived first in the Flex queue runs first.
- SMED keeps changeovers short enough that the wheel can turn frequently (every 2–3 days instead of weekly).

Why It Works: The Wheel handles 80% of your volume with predictable scheduling. The Flex Slot absorbs the 20% chaos without breaking the system. SMED makes the whole thing economically viable by keeping changeover penalties low.

Example: Your heat treat oven runs five families on a 3-day wheel. Families A through E each have assigned windows proportional to demand. Friday afternoon is the Flex Slot for prototypes and oddball orders. SMED has gotten changeovers to 15 minutes, so you can afford five setups per rotation without losing a full shift.

When to Avoid: If your demand is highly variable week to week (busiest week is more than 2x the slowest week), the fixed wheel will constantly need overriding. Use Combination 2 instead.

Combination 2: FIFO + Ticket System + SMED

Best For: High variability. True job shop behavior where the mix changes weekly. Many unique or low-repeat jobs.

How It Works:

- FIFO with Priority Rules determines the sequence. Jobs run in the order they arrive, with Red and Yellow tags for genuine emergencies.
- The Ticket System (CONWIP) caps WIP (See the full Ticket System explanation and

diagram in Chapter 5). Cells cannot flood the monument because they need a physical Ticket to release work. No Ticket, no release.

- SMED keeps changeovers short so that small-batch FIFO processing is economically viable.

Why It Works: FIFO handles unpredictable demand without requiring a fixed schedule. The Ticket System prevents the FIFO lane from becoming an infinite queue. SMED ensures you can run small batches without burning half your capacity on setups.

Example: Your CNC machining center processes parts from four cells. Demand shifts weekly based on customer orders. Each cell has three Tickets. When a cell finishes a batch and attaches a Ticket, the Water Strider moves it to the FIFO lane. The monument processes jobs in arrival order. When the batch is done, the Ticket returns to the cell, authorizing the next release. Total WIP at the monument is capped at 12 batches (4 cells x 3 Tickets) at all times.

When to Avoid: If you have clear product families with repeatable demand, you are leaving optimization on the table. A Campaign Wheel would give you better changeover sequencing than pure FIFO.

Combination 3: Time-Slicing + Supermarket + SMED

Best For: High utilization (>75%). Multiple cells competing for access. A significant portion of demand is repetitive (runners).

How It Works:

- Time-Slicing gives each cell a guaranteed access window. Cell A runs from 6–10 AM, Cell B from 10 AM–2 PM, Cell C from 2–6 PM.
- Supermarkets buffer the top 20% of products (your runners). These standard parts are pre-built and stocked so that downstream cells are never waiting on the monument for common items.
- SMED ensures changeovers between windows are fast enough that the time lost during cell-to-cell transitions is minimal.

Why It Works: Time-Slicing eliminates the political fight for machine time. Supermarkets offload the highest-volume work so the monument's limited time is focused on the variable, custom work that actually needs scheduling. SMED makes the transitions between time slots efficient.

Example: Three machining cells share a plating line. Cell A has the 6–10 AM window. But 30% of Cell A's output is the same five standard housings every week. Those housings are built to a Supermarket—Cell A runs them during slack time, and downstream pulls from the buffer. This means Cell A's monument window is freed up for its custom and low-volume work, effectively increasing available capacity without buying anything.

When to Avoid: If utilization is below 60%, Time-Slicing adds unnecessary rigidity. You have enough capacity that cells do not need dedicated windows—use Combination 1 or 2 instead.

The Decision Matrix

Use this to select your starting combination.

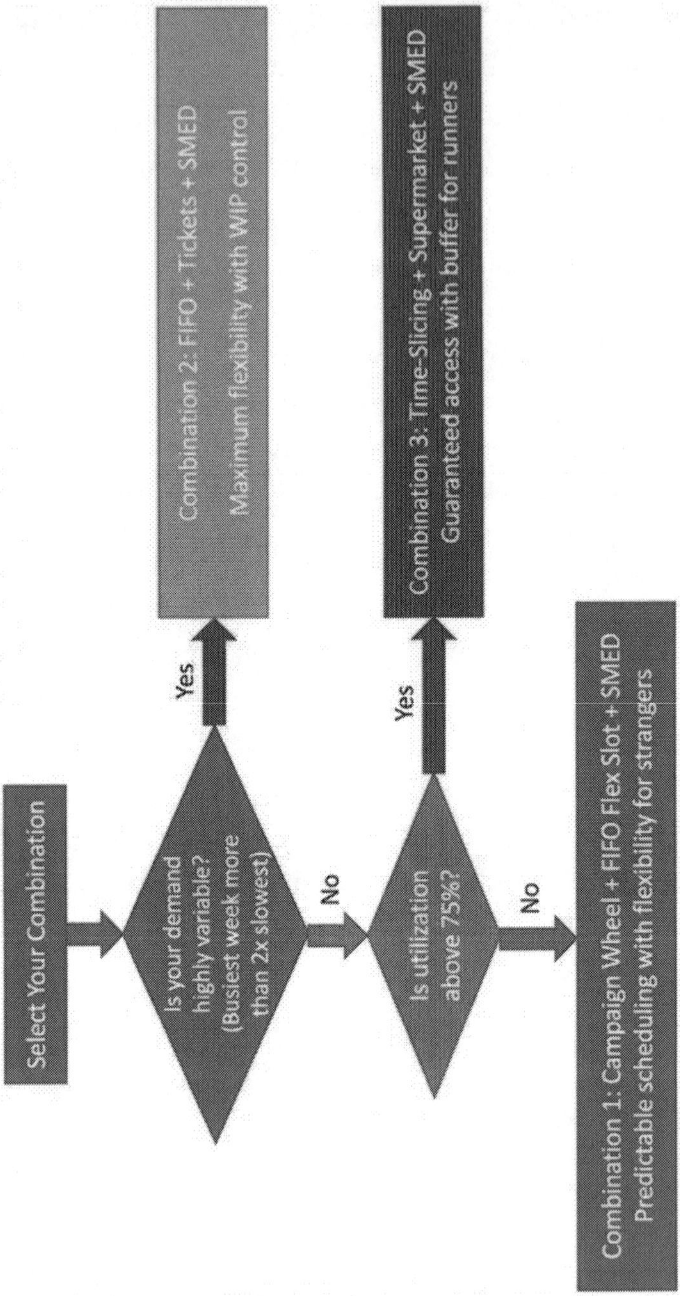
Select Your Combination
Is your demand highly variable? (Busiest week more than 2x slowest)
Yes
Combination 2: FIFO + Tickets + SMED
Maximum flexibility with WIP control
No
Is utilization above 75%?
Yes
Combination 3: Time-Slicing + Supermarket + SMED
Guaranteed access with buffer for runners
No
Combination 1: Campaign Wheel + FIFO Flex Slot + SMED
Predictable scheduling with flexibility for strangers

Your Situation	Utilization	Demand Pattern	Start With
Moderate load, repeatable families, some strangers	50–75%	Stable (±30%)	Combination 1: Wheel + FIFO Flex + SMED
High variability, true job shop, few repeats	Any	Variable (>2x swing)	Combination 2: FIFO + Tickets + SMED
Heavy load, cells fighting for access, some runners	>75%	Mixed (runners + custom)	Combination 3: Time-Slice + Supermarket + SMED

Notice that SMED appears in every combination. This is not a coincidence. Changeover reduction is the universal enabler. Without short setups, none of the scheduling strategies are economically viable because the batch sizes required to amortize long changeovers will destroy flow regardless of how clever your scheduling is.

If you have not done a SMED event on your constraint, stop here and go to Book 2. Come back when changeovers are under 30 minutes.

Layering: Adding Strategies Over Time

You do not need to implement all elements of your combination on Day 1. Layer them in using the 60-Day Roadmap from Chapter 7.

A typical layering sequence:

- **Days 1–14:** SMED + Release Rules (Gatekeeper Checklist). This is always first. You cannot schedule what you cannot change over quickly, and you cannot manage flow if incomplete work is flooding the queue.
- **Days 15–28:** Add your primary scheduling strategy (Wheel, FIFO, or Time-Slicing). The Water Strider launches during this phase.

- **Days 29–42:** Add the WIP control mechanism (Tickets for Combination 2, Supermarkets for Combination 3, or the Flex Slot rules for Combination 1).
- **Days 43–60:** Audit, adjust, and refine. Use the Monument Scorecard to identify which element needs tuning.

When to Switch Combinations

Your starting combination is not permanent. As conditions change, you may need to evolve.

Signals that you need to shift:

- **Wheel → FIFO:** Your product mix is changing faster than the wheel can adapt. Monthly wheel adjustments are not keeping up. More than 25% of volume is hitting the Flex Slot.
- **FIFO → Wheel:** Your mix has stabilized. You notice the same families running every week in roughly the same proportions. A wheel would eliminate redundant changeovers.

- **Time-Slicing → Wheel or FIFO:** Utilization has dropped (maybe you added a shift or demand softened). The fixed windows are creating idle time. Switch to a more flexible approach.

- **Any → Add Supermarket:** You keep running the same 5–10 parts through the constraint every week. Pull them out of the scheduling system entirely and buffer them.

The key: review your combination quarterly using the Monument Scorecard data (Chapter 7). If the Expedite Rate is climbing or Buffer Health is deteriorating, your current combination may no longer fit your reality.

Common Mistakes

1. **Using all six strategies at once.** This is not a buffet. More strategies means more rules, more training, and more ways to fail. Pick two or three. Master them. Add complexity only when the data tells you the current system is insufficient.

2. **Skipping SMED.** Every combination assumes changeovers are reasonable. If your

setup times are still high, no scheduling strategy will save you. Fix the foundation first.

3. **Forcing a Wheel on a job shop.** If your demand genuinely changes every week and you have 200 unique SKUs with no repeatable families, a Campaign Wheel is the wrong tool. Use FIFO with Tickets and accept the variability.

4. **Ignoring the transition cost.** Switching from one combination to another mid-stream is disruptive. Do not change strategies every month because the latest metric dipped. Give each combination 90 days to stabilize before evaluating.

To see how one shop combined these strategies and transformed a chaotic heat treat oven into a predictable, managed constraint, see the full Precision Components case study in Appendix B.

Start Here If You're Not Sure

If you have read through the six strategies and three combinations and still feel uncertain, use these three plain-language rules:

- "My demand is all over the place and every week looks different."
  - Start with Combination 2: FIFO + Tickets + SMED.
- "I keep running the same families every week in roughly the same proportions."
  - Start with Combination 1: Campaign Wheel + FIFO Flex Slot + SMED.
- "My cells are fighting for access to the machine and everyone is frustrated."
  - Start with Combination 3: Time-Slicing + Supermarket + SMED.

All three start with SMED and Release Rules in Week 1. The only question is which scheduling approach you layer on top.

Chapter 4

Cell Design Around Monuments

Traditional Lean says "put the machine in the cell." But you can't put one massive heat treat oven into three different cells. You must design your cells to hand work off to the monument and get it back without losing flow.

Pattern 1: The Incomplete Cell (Most Common)

The cell contains all operations *except* the monument.

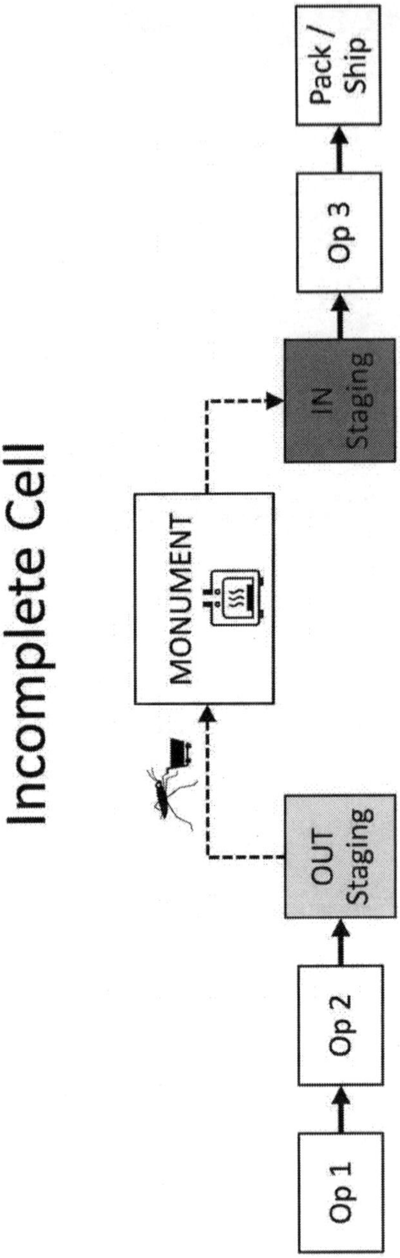
Incomplete Cell
Op 1
Op 2
OUT Staging
MONUMENT
IN Staging
Op 3
Pack / Ship

- **Flow:** Op 1 → Op 2 → **OUT Staging** → Monument → **IN Staging** → Op 3 → Pack.
- **Key Feature:** The cell has specific, marked "OUT" and "IN" squares on the floor. This visually tracks WIP leaving and returning.

Pattern 2: Hybrid Cells

Use this when you have a "High Runner" product family (Pareto principle).

- **High Volume Family:** Invest in a dedicated, smaller machine *inside* their cell.
- **Low Volume Families:** Continue to share the centralized monument.
- **Why:** This unloads the shared resource and gives your biggest product perfect flow.

Pattern 3: Central Monument with Radial Cells

If you are rearranging the factory, place the monument in the center and arrange cells like spokes on a wheel.

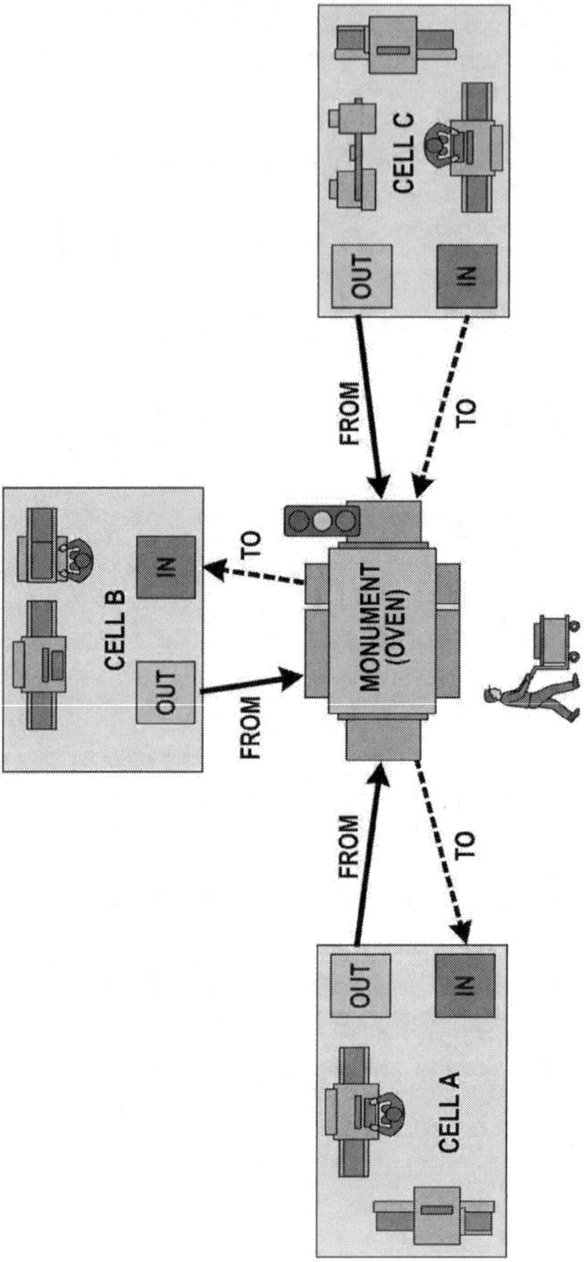
CELL C
OUT
IN
FROM
TO
CELL B
IN
OUT
TO
FROM
MONUMENT
(OVEN)
FROM
TO
CELL A
OUT
IN

- **Benefit:** Minimizes transport time for everyone.
- **Requirement:** Visual management must be high (tower lights, large screens) so all cells can see the monument's status from their desks.

Operator Choreography: Who Runs It?

Design isn't just layout; it's labor.

Model A: Dedicated Operator

- **Best For:** Complex equipment (e.g., heat treat) or high utilization.
- **Rule:** This operator *never* leaves the monument. They do not fetch parts. They process only.

Model B: The Water Strider (The Feeder)

- **Concept**: A dedicated material handler runs a fixed route between cells and the monument. They move completed work from Cell OUT squares to the Monument IN queue / buffer, return finished parts to Cell IN squares, and serve as the Gatekeeper—

rejecting any batch that fails the release checklist.

- **The Prime Directive**: "The Monument Never Stops Eating." The Water Strider ensures the monument's input buffer is always topped off.
- This role is critical enough that it requires its own standard work, training protocol, and backup plan. For the complete Water Strider playbook—including route design, escalation triggers, selection criteria, and a printable standard work template (see Chapter 6, Layer 5).

Model C: Cell Operators (Time-Slicing)

- **Best For:** Simple equipment, low utilization.
- **Rule:** Cell A's operator walks over during their 10:00 AM window, runs their parts, and returns.

The No-Fly Zone (Safety & Discipline)

Paint a red line or box around the shared equipment (approx. 10 feet).

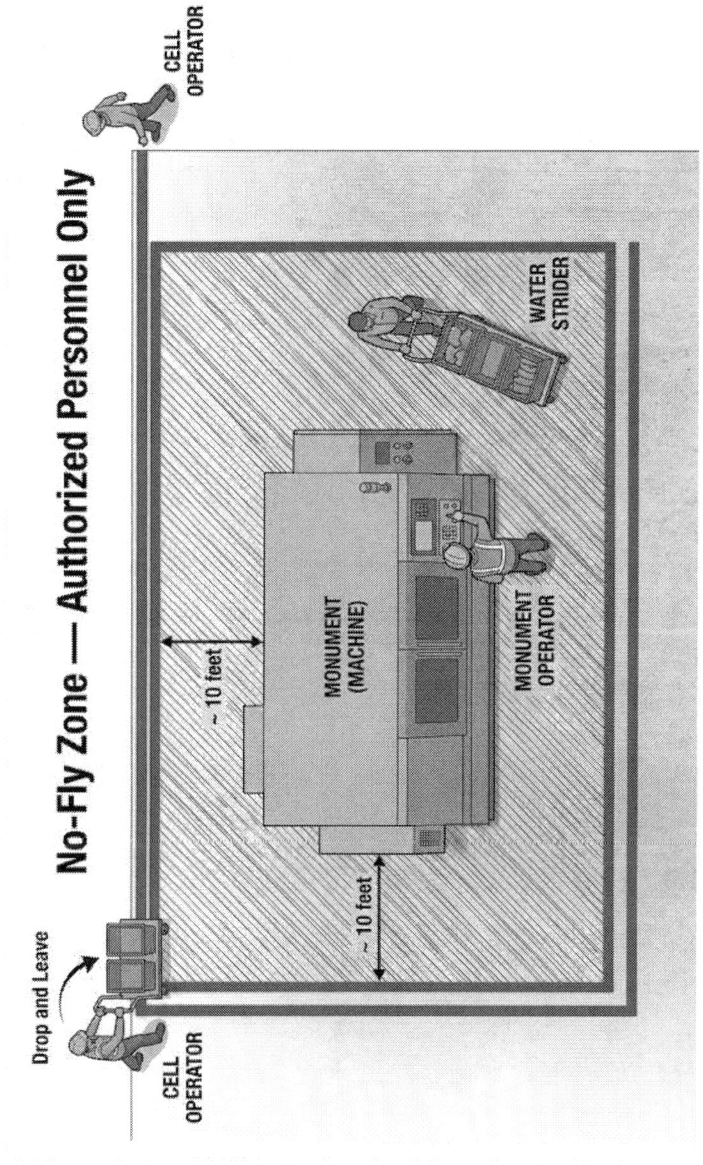

No-Fly Zone — Authorized Personnel Only
CELL OPERATOR
Drop and Leave
CELL OPERATOR
~ 10 feet
~ 10 feet
MONUMENT (MACHINE)
MONUMENT OPERATOR
WATER STRIDER

- **Rule:** Only the Monument Operator and Water Strider may enter the Red Zone.
- **Why:** It prevents cell operators from "helping" (hovering, interrupting, or trying to jump the queue). They drop work at the line and leave.

Visual Management: Buffer Zone Rule

You cannot manage what you cannot see. Mark a Warning Line at 50% of the buffer and a Red Line at 25% of the buffer on the input rack or wall.

- **Above the Warning Line:** Green. System is healthy.
- **At or below the Warning Line:** Water Strider checks upstream for delays.
- **At or below the Red Line:** Immediate escalation to Water Strider/Supervisor.

*See **Appendix A** for the **Cell Design Worksheet**.*

Chapter 5

Material Flow and Scheduling

You have a layout (Chapter 4). Now you need a nervous system.

If the layout is the *skeleton*, material flow is the *blood*. It brings work to the constraint exactly when needed...not too early (flooding) and not too late (starvation).

The Two-Buffer System

Unlike a standard cell where flow is continuous, a shared monument requires **two distinct buffers** with different purposes.

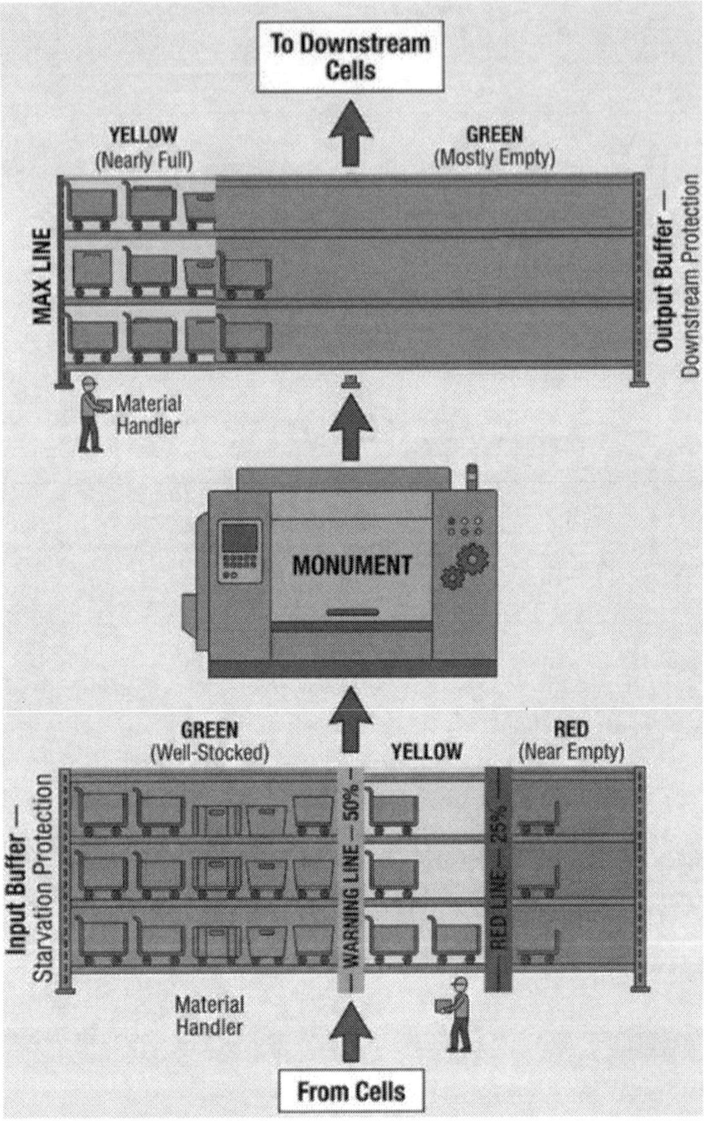
To Downstream Cells
YELLOW
(Nearly Full)
GREEN
(Mostly Empty)
MAX LINE
Output Buffer —
Downstream Protection
Material Handler
MONUMENT
GREEN
(Well-Stocked)
YELLOW
RED
(Near Empty)
Input Buffer —
Starvation Protection
— WARNING LINE — 50% —
RED LINE — 25% —
Material Handler
From Cells

1. The Input Buffer (Starvation Protection)

- **Purpose:** Ensures the monument *never* stops for lack of work, even if an upstream cell breaks down.
- **Target Size:** 4–8 hours of work.
- **The "Warning Line" Rule:** Mark a yellow Warning Line at the 50% buffer mark. If inventory drops below this line, the Water Strider checks upstream cells for delays.
- **The "Red Line" Rule:** Mark a red line at the 25% buffer mark. If inventory drops below this line, it is an immediate "Andon" event. The Water Strider and Supervisor must react immediately.

2. The Output Buffer (Downstream Protection)

- **Purpose:** Ensures downstream cells keep running even if the monument breaks down.
- **Target Size:** Determined by the monument's repair lead time (usually 4–12 hours).

- **Warning:** If this buffer is full, the monument **MUST STOP**. Do not keep running just to stay busy.

Simplified Buffer Sizing for Shared Equipment

Earlier in this chapter, we introduced the Two-Buffer System: an Input Buffer to prevent starvation and an Output Buffer to protect downstream cells. We referenced Book 5 (Material Flow) for detailed calculations.

But not everyone has read Book 5. And even if you have, you do not need a spreadsheet to get started. You need a napkin.

This section gives you a quick-calculation method to size both buffers well enough to launch. You can refine later with the full methodology in Book 5. A buffer that is roughly right today is infinitely better than a perfectly calculated buffer that takes three weeks to design.

The Purpose of a Buffer (A 30-Second Refresher)

A buffer exists to absorb variability. That is its only job.

Your cells do not produce at a perfectly constant rate. Your monument does not run without interruption. Demand does not arrive in neat, predictable waves. The buffer is the shock absorber between these imperfect realities.

Too small: The monument starves when a cell has a bad hour. Flow stops. Too large: You are hiding problems behind mountains of inventory. Lead time bloats.

The goal is the smallest buffer that prevents starvation 95% of the time.

Input Buffer Sizing: The Quick Calc

The Input Buffer sits between the cells and the monument. Its job is to keep the monument fed even when upstream hiccups occur.

You need two numbers:

1. **Replenishment Time:** How long does it take to get more work to the monument after the buffer starts draining? This is not the cell's cycle time. It is the realistic time from "cell finishes a batch" to "Water Strider

delivers it to the monument's Input Buffer." Include the route frequency.

2. **Variability Factor:** How unreliable are your upstream cells?

The Formula:

Input Buffer = Replenishment Time x Variability Factor

The Variability Factor:

Upstream Reliability	Factor	Use When...
Stable	1.5x	Cells rarely stop. Staffing is consistent. Few quality issues.
Moderate	2.0x	Occasional breakdowns. Some absenteeism. Rework happens weekly.
Unstable	3.0x	Frequent stoppages. High absenteeism. Quality problems are common.

These multipliers are not sacred. They are practical starting bands for manual systems. Use them to launch quickly, then tune the buffer with real scorecard data over the first 30 days.

Example:

Your Water Strider runs a 45-minute route. A cell typically finishes a batch every 60 minutes. So the realistic replenishment time from "buffer starts draining" to "new work arrives" is roughly 105 minutes (one cell cycle + one Water Strider route, worst case).

Your cells are moderately reliable—they have occasional issues but nothing catastrophic. Variability Factor: 2.0x.

Input Buffer = 105 minutes × 2.0 = 210 minutes = 3.5 hours of work.

Round up to the nearest practical unit. If the monument processes full carts and each cart takes 45 minutes to run, 3.5 hours rounds up to 5 carts. Your Input Buffer is 5 carts.

The Warning Line and Red Line: Mark the Warning Line at 50% of the input buffer and the Red Line at 25% of the input buffer. In this case, the Warning

Line is at 2-3 carts — when the buffer drops here, the Water Strider checks upstream for delays. The Red Line is at 1-2 carts — when the buffer drops here, escalate immediately.

Output Buffer Sizing: The Quick Calc

The Output Buffer sits between the monument and the downstream cells. Its job is to keep downstream cells running even when the monument stops unexpectedly.

You need two numbers:

1. **Recovery Time:** How long does it take to get the monument running again after an unplanned stop? Do not use the average. Use the 80th percentile—the repair time you hit 80% of the time. If 8 out of 10 breakdowns are fixed within 2 hours but the other 2 take a full shift, your Recovery Time is 2 hours — the 80th percentile, not the average time of 3.2 hours.

2. **Downstream Consumption Rate:** How fast do downstream cells consume work from the Output Buffer? Measure in the same units (carts, totes, batches per hour).

The Formula:

Output Buffer = Recovery Time × Downstream Consumption Rate

Example:

Your monument (the heat treat oven) breaks down occasionally. Looking at the last three months of maintenance logs, 80% of breakdowns are resolved within 2 hours.

Downstream cells consume approximately 1.5 carts per hour from the Output Buffer.

Output Buffer = 2 hours × 1.5 carts/hour = 3 carts.

The MAX Line: Your Output Buffer also needs a ceiling. If the buffer is full, the monument must stop—even if it could keep running. This feels wrong. Every instinct will tell you to keep the machine busy. Resist. An overflowing Output Buffer means you are building inventory that downstream does not need, which means you are consuming capacity that another family needs.

A practical starting point is to set the MAX Line at about 1.5x the calculated output buffer, then adjust once you see actual downstream pull behavior. In this case, 1.5 × 3 carts = 4.5, rounded to 5 carts. If the Output Buffer hits 5 carts, the monument stops and waits.

The calculated buffer (3 carts) is what you need. The MAX Line (5 carts) is where overproduction starts. The gap between them is breathing room.

Note: Size the buffer by total volume, not per part number. The buffer holds whatever the monument is processing, regardless of which part number is running.

The Buffer Sizing Cheat Sheet

For those who want the answer without the math:

Buffer	Conservative Start	Refine Later
Input Buffer	4–8 hours of work	Adjust down as reliability improves
Input Red Line	25% of the Input Buffer	Triggers immediate escalation

Buffer	Conservative Start	Refine Later
Output Buffer	Equal to monument repair time	Use 80th percentile, not average
Output MAX Line	1.5x the Output Buffer	Monument stops when full

If you are launching tomorrow and cannot measure anything, start with a 6-hour Input Buffer and an Output Buffer equal to one shift of downstream consumption. You will be wrong, but you will be close enough to learn. Adjust weekly using the Buffer Health metric on the Monument Scorecard.

Reading the Buffer: Green, Yellow, Red

Once your buffers are sized, divide them into zones for visual management.

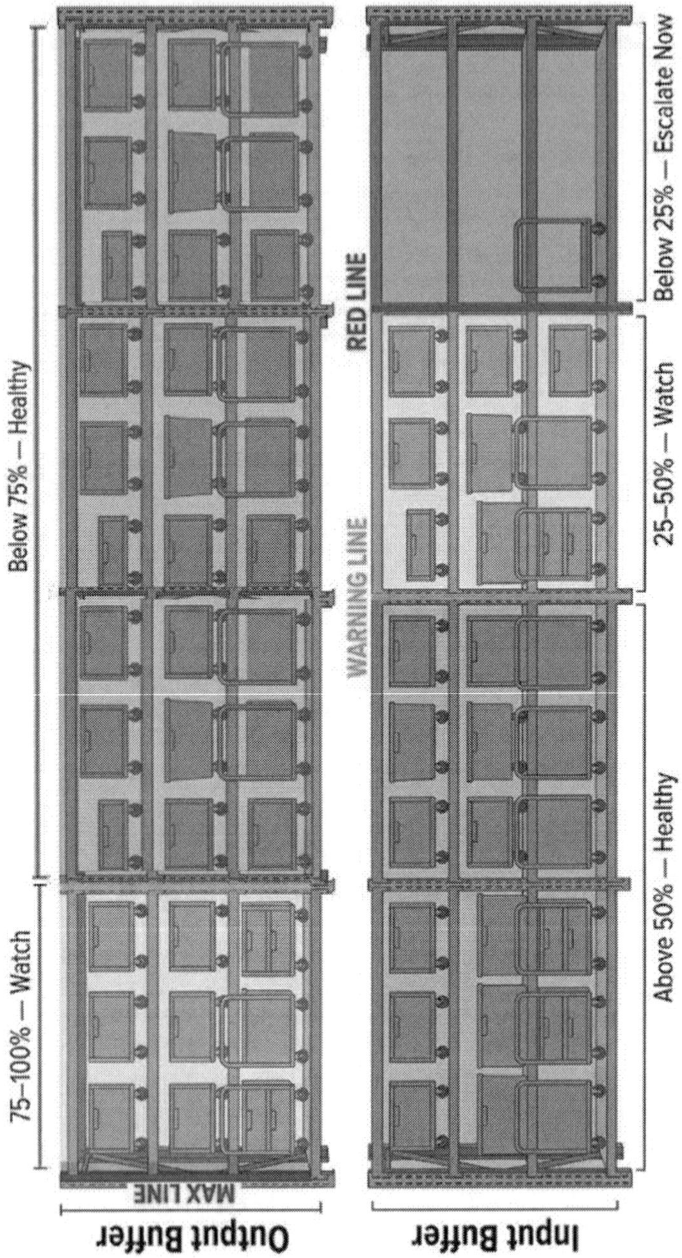
Output Buffer
MAX LINE
75–100% — Watch
Below 75% — Healthy
WARNING LINE
RED LINE
Input Buffer
Above 50% — Healthy
25–50% — Watch
Below 25% — Escalate Now

Input Buffer Zones:

Zone	Level	Meaning	Action
Green	Above 50% full	Healthy. *Monument is well-fed.*	No action. Continue normal operations.
Yellow	25–50% full	Watch. *Replenishment may be slowing.*	Water Strider checks upstream cells for delays.
Red	Below 25% full (at or below the Red Line)	Starvation risk.	Immediate escalation. Supervisor intervenes.

Output Buffer Zones:

Zone	Level	Meaning	Action
Green	Below 75% full	Healthy. *Downstream is pulling normally.*	No action.
Yellow	75–100% full	Watch. *Downstream may be slowing.*	Water Strider checks downstream cells for issues.
Red	At MAX Line	Full. *Monument must stop.*	Monument pauses. Investigate downstream blockage.

Mark these zones directly on the wall, rack, or floor next to the buffer. Use green, yellow, and red tape. The Water Strider logs which zone the buffer is in at every route stop (Stop 9 on the Standard Work template). This data feeds the Buffer Health metric on the Monument Scorecard.

Adjusting Buffers Over Time

Your initial buffer sizes are educated guesses. They will be wrong. That is fine. Use the Monument Scorecard data to refine.

After 30 days, ask two questions:

1. How often was the Input Buffer in the Red Zone?
    - More than 20% of checks: Buffer is too small. Increase by 25%.
    - Less than 5% of checks: Buffer may be too large. Decrease by 25%.
    - Between 5–20%: Buffer is sized correctly. Leave it alone.
2. How often was the Output Buffer at MAX?
    - More than 20% of checks: Downstream cannot keep up. Investigate the downstream constraint before increasing the buffer.

  - Less than 5%: Buffer may be too large. You are carrying unnecessary inventory. Decrease by 25%.
  - Between 5–20%: Buffer is sized correctly.

Adjust in small increments. A 25% change is enough to see the effect without destabilizing the system. Never adjust both buffers simultaneously—change one, observe for two weeks, then evaluate the other.

One diagnostic to watch for: if you are constantly in the Red Zone on the Input Buffer AND constantly at the MAX Line on the Output Buffer at the same time, your issue is the monument's capacity, not scheduling. The strategies in this book optimize flow — they cannot create capacity that does not exist. Go back to Chapter 2 and re-run the Constraint Type Test.

Common Mistakes

1. **Using averages for everything.** Averages hide the spikes that actually starve your monument. A cell that averages 1 cart per hour but occasionally goes 3 hours

without output will starve a buffer sized to the average. Use the Variability Factor to account for this.

2. **Sizing the Output Buffer to zero.** Some managers refuse to allow inventory after the monument because "inventory is waste." In a perfect world, yes. In a world where the monument breaks down, zero output buffer means downstream stops every time the monument hiccups. The buffer is the lesser waste.

3. **Never adjusting.** The buffer you set on Day 1 should not be the buffer you have on Day 180. As reliability improves (fewer cell stoppages, fewer monument breakdowns), your buffers should shrink. Shrinking buffers is a sign of a maturing system.

4. **Treating the MAX Line as optional.** When the Output Buffer is full and the monument is still running, someone will say, "But the machine is open—why would we stop it?" Because running parts that downstream cannot consume is not production. It is overproduction, the worst

of the seven wastes. The MAX Line is not a suggestion.

Scheduling: The Heartbeat

The constraint sets the pace for the entire plant. We call this the **Heartbeat**.

Heartbeat = Average Process Cycle + Average Changeover

- **Example:** 75-minute heat treat cycle + 15-minute changeover = **90-minute Heartbeat**.

Synchronization Rules:

- **Water Strider**: Runs a fixed route every half-heartbeat (e.g., every 45 minutes on a 90-minute heartbeat). This route covers every Cell OUT square, the Monument IN buffer, the Monument OUT buffer, and every Cell IN square. The route frequency is non-negotiable—it is the pulse that keeps the system alive. See Chapter 6, Layer 5 for the full route design and standard work template.

- **Cell Batches:** Cells should produce in multiples of the heartbeat (e.g., one full oven load).
- **Visuals**: The countdown timer on the monument drives the rhythm of the shop.

The FIFO vs. Supermarket Decision

Should you use a FIFO lane or a Supermarket?

Feature	FIFO Lane	Supermarket
Best For	Custom / Make-to-Order	Repetitive / Make-to-Stock
Sequence	Fixed (First In, First Out)	Flexible (Pick what is needed)
Constraint	Physical Lane (Roller conveyor)	Bin/Rack System
Logic	"Process the next job."	"Refill the empty bin."

The HMLV Hybrid Rule:

Most shops need both.

- **Top 20% "Runners":** Use a **Supermarket**. Keep a stock of standard shafts/housings ready to go.
- **Bottom 80% "Strangers":** Use a **FIFO Lane**. Process them in the order they arrive.

The Ticket System (CONWIP)

How do you prevent cells from flooding the Input Buffer and monument with work? **The Ticket System.**

This is a physical limit on Work-In-Process (WIP). It prevents the "Phantom Backlog" where work sits in the Input Buffer for weeks.

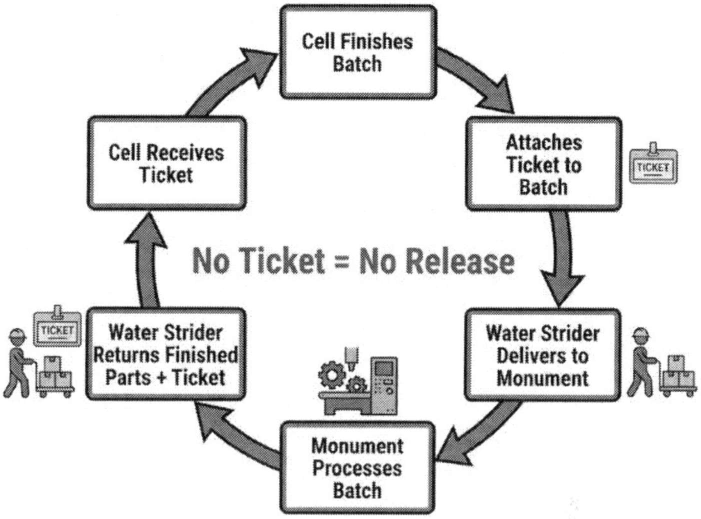

How it works:

1. **The Constraint:** Allocate a specific number of "Tickets" (laminated cards or magnetic tokens) based on the buffer size.
   - *Example:* The Oven Input Buffer holds 10 carts. There are exactly 10 Tickets in circulation.
2. **The Rule:** A cell *cannot* release a job to the monument's queue / Input Buffer unless they have a Ticket to attach to it.

3. **The Loop:**

   - Cell finishes a batch →Attaches Ticket →Water Strider takes to Monument.
   - Monument runs batch → Water Strider returns finished parts on the next route → Ticket travels back to Cell.
   - Cell receives Ticket → Allowed to release next batch.

No Ticket = No Release. If there is no ticket, the cell must stop and do 5S, maintenance, training, etc. This is the hardest discipline to learn, but it eliminates the chaotic pile-up of WIP.

The behavior change is immediate. Before Tickets: 18 carts jammed in the aisle with no one knowing what runs next. After Tickets: a maximum of 10 batches in circulation, cells doing productive maintenance when they have no Ticket, and the monument processing work in a calm, predictable sequence.

Chapter 6

Standard Work for Shared Equipment

Standard work for a standalone cell is about *motion*. Standard work for a monument is about *handoffs*.

Because multiple teams interact with this machine, the errors happen in the gaps between them.

Layer 1: The Three Non-Negotiables

Before you write a single page of SOPs, post these three rules on the machine.

1. No Incomplete Kits.

Never load the input buffer with partial work. If it is missing a traveler, a tool, or a part, it stays in the cell.

2. No Undocumented Changeovers.

Every setup is timed and logged. If you don't log it, it didn't happen.

3. No Running Without a Recipe.

The recipe must be verified against the traveler *before* the cycle start button is pressed.

Layer 2: Handoff Protocols (RACI)

This is where you define who owns the part at every millisecond.

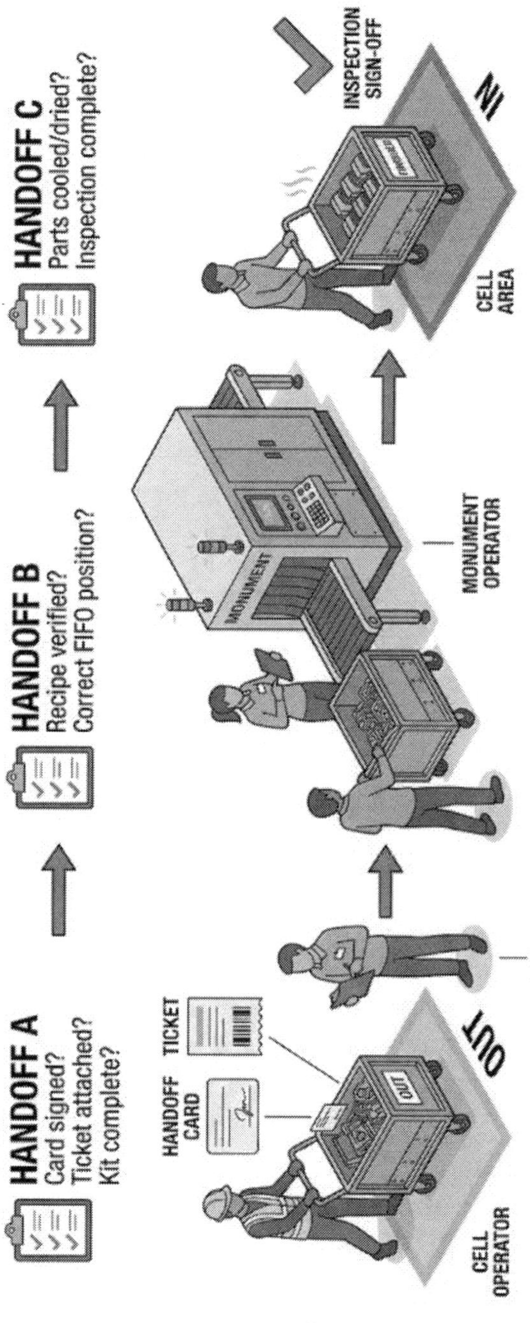
HANDOFF A
Card signed?
Ticket attached?
Kit complete?
HANDOFF B
Recipe verified?
Correct FIFO position?
HANDOFF C
Parts cooled/dried?
Inspection complete?
HANDOFF CARD
TICKET
OUT
CELL OPERATOR
WATER STRIDER
MONUMENT
MONUMENT OPERATOR
INSPECTION SIGN-OFF
IN
CELL AREA

Handoff A: Cell → Water Strider

- **Location:** Cell "OUT" Square.
- **Requirement:** Handoff Card signed by Cell Operator. Ticket attached.
- **Gatekeeper:** The Water Strider checks the card. If the paperwork is wrong, they **reject** the load. The Cell Operator must fix it. *The Water Strider has absolute authority here.*

Handoff B: Water Strider → Monument

- **Location:** Monument "IN" Buffer.
- **Requirement:** Parts placed in the correct FIFO lane or family grouping.
- **Check:** Monument Operator verifies recipe compatibility before accepting.

Handoff C: Monument → Cell

- **Location:** Cell "IN" Square.
- **Requirement:** Parts cooled/dried. Post-process inspection sign-off complete.

Layer 3: The Downtime Playbook

When a monument goes down, you cannot afford 20 minutes of confusion. You need a "Communication Burst."

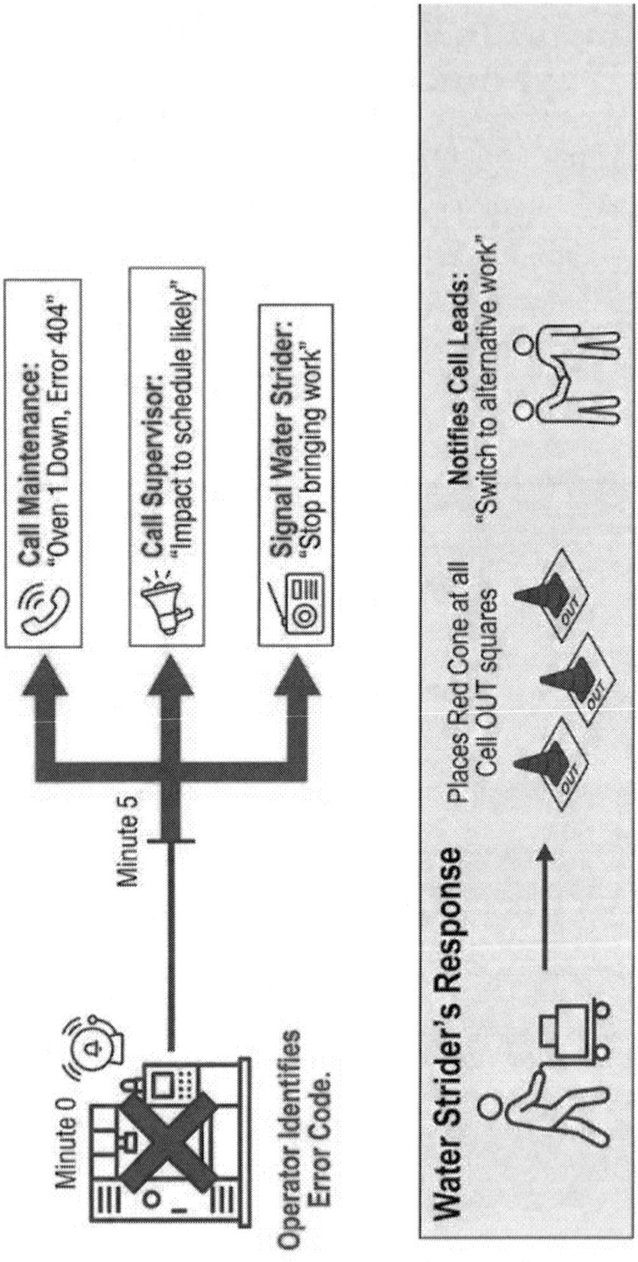

Minute 0
Operator Identifies Error Code.
Minute 5
Call Maintenance:
“Oven 1 Down, Error 404”
Call Supervisor:
“Impact to schedule likely”
Signal Water Strider:
“Stop bringing work”
Water Strider's Response
Places Red Cone at all Cell OUT squares
OUT
OUT
OUT
Notifies Cell Leads:
“Switch to alternative work”

The Playbook:

1. **Minute 0:** Operator identifies error code.
2. **Minute 5:** If not fixed, initiate Communication Burst:
    - **Call Maintenance:** "Oven 1 Down, Error 404."
    - **Call Supervisor:** "Impact to schedule likely."
    - **Signal Water Strider:** "Stop bringing work." The Water Strider places a Red Cone at every Cell OUT square and notifies Cell Leads to switch to alternative work. See Layer 5 for the full escalation protocol.

Layer 4: Changeover Audits

You did the SMED event in Chapter 3. Now you must sustain it.

The Sustainment System:

- **Shadow Boards:** Tools are not in a drawer; they are outlined on a board. If a spot is empty, the machine does not run until it is found.

- **Pre-Flight Checklist:** External tasks (staging the next cart, finding the new recipe) must be done *while the machine is running*.
- **The Audit:** Once a week, the supervisor watches a changeover with a stopwatch.
    - *Target:* 20 Minutes.
        - *Actual:* 22 Minutes.
            - *Action:* Good.
        - *Actual:* 35 Minutes.
            - *Action:* Immediate root cause analysis. Why did we drift?

Layer 5: Water Strider Standard Work

The Water Strider is arguably the most important role in a shared equipment system. They are not a material handler. They are the nervous system of the constraint—the single person responsible for ensuring the monument never starves, never floods, and never processes bad work.

The name comes from the insect that skates across the surface of water, touching every part of the pond without sinking. Your Water Strider touches every cell, every buffer, and the monument itself on a fixed route, at a fixed frequency, without getting pulled into firefighting.

If you take one thing from this book, take this: The Water Strider role is the difference between a system that works on paper and a system that works on the floor.

Why a Dedicated Role?

In most plants, material movement to the monument happens one of three ways:

1. Cell operators walk parts over "when they get a chance." (Translation: parts sit for hours.)
2. A forklift driver grabs whatever is closest. (Translation: FIFO is destroyed.)
3. A supervisor physically carries parts during a crisis. (Translation: the supervisor is not supervising.)

All three approaches fail because no single person owns the flow. The Water Strider fixes this by creating a single point of accountability.

The Three Jobs

The Water Strider has exactly three responsibilities. Not four. Not seven. Three.

Job 1: Feed the Monument

The constraint never stops eating. The Water Strider ensures the Input Buffer stays in the Green Zone (above 50%) at all times. They move completed work from Cell OUT squares to the Monument IN buffer on a fixed route.

If the buffer drops below the Warning Line (50%), the Water Strider checks upstream cells for delays. If it drops below the Red Line (25%), it is an immediate escalation—not in 30 minutes, not at the next break. Now.

Job 2: Guard the Gate

The Water Strider is the Gatekeeper. They inspect every batch before it enters the monument input buffer using the Gatekeeper Checklist (Appendix A, Tool 2).

- Traveler attached? Check.
- All parts present? Check.
- Recipe specified? Check.
- Handoff Card signed by the Cell Operator? Check.

If any box is unchecked, the Water Strider rejects the batch. It goes back to the cell. No exceptions. No "I'll bring the paperwork in a minute." No "just run it, we'll figure it out later."

This is where the role gets hard. Cell operators will push back. Supervisors will pressure. The Water Strider must have the authority—backed by the Plant Manager—to reject incomplete work. If they lose this authority even once, the gate is broken and every shortcut returns within a week.

Job 3: Return Finished Work

After the monument completes processing, the Water Strider moves finished parts from the Monument OUT area back to the correct Cell IN square. They complete Section C of the Handoff Card, noting the total lead time through the constraint.

This closes the loop. The Ticket attached to that batch is now free, which signals the cell that they may release their next batch.

The Fixed Route

The Water Strider runs a fixed route at a fixed interval. The interval is tied to the Heartbeat of the constraint.

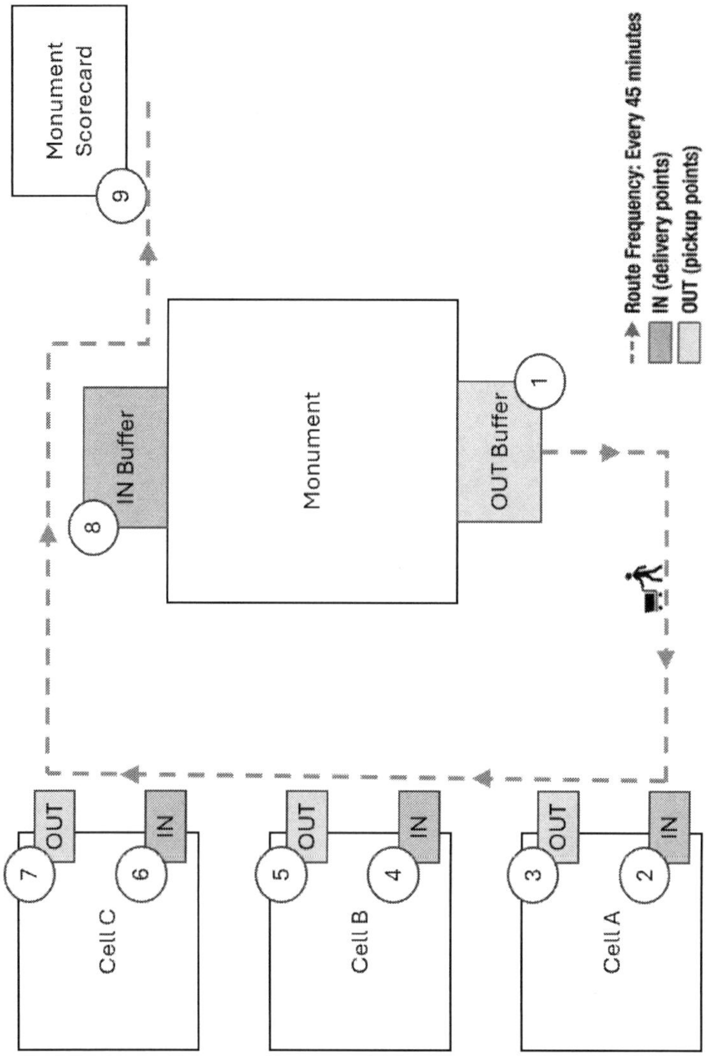
Monument Scorecard
9
IN Buffer
8
Monument
OUT Buffer
1
Cell C
OUT
7
IN
6
Cell B
OUT
5
IN
4
Cell A
OUT
3
IN
2
Route Frequency: Every 45 minutes
IN (delivery points)
OUT (pickup points)

Route Frequency: Every half-heartbeat.

If the monument has a 90-minute heartbeat (75-minute cycle + 15-minute changeover), the Water Strider completes a full route every 45 minutes.

The Route Sequence:

Stop	Location	Action	Time
1	Monument OUT Buffer	Pick up finished parts. Collect freed Tickets.	5 min
2	Cell A IN Square	Deliver finished parts to Cell A. Return Ticket.	3 min
3	Cell A OUT Square	Check for completed work. Inspect Handoff Card. Load if ready.	5 min
4	Cell B IN Square	Deliver finished parts to Cell B. Return Ticket.	3 min
5	Cell B OUT Square	Check for completed work. Inspect Handoff Card. Load if ready.	5 min

Stop	Location	Action	Time
6	Cell C IN Square	Deliver finished parts to Cell C. Return Ticket.	3 min
7	Cell C OUT Square	Check for completed work. Inspect Handoff Card. Load if ready.	5 min
8	Monument IN Buffer	Deliver new work. Check buffer level against Warning Line /Red Line.	5 min
9	Monument Scorecard	Update Buffer Health check (Green/Yellow/Red).	2 min
—	**Total Route Time**		**~36 min**

That leaves approximately 9 minutes of slack in a 45-minute cycle. This slack is intentional—it absorbs the variability of real life (a cart with a stuck wheel, a question from an operator, a bathroom break).

Do not fill this slack with additional tasks. The Water Strider is not a general-purpose material handler. If you load them with other duties, the route will slip, the buffer will starve, and the system collapses.

The Escalation Protocol

The Water Strider is the early warning system. They see problems before anyone else because they are physically present at every handoff point every 45 minutes.

Condition 1: Input Buffer Below Red Line (Starvation Risk)

- Water Strider Action: Immediately notify the Supervisor. Place a Red Cone at the monument.
- Supervisor Action: Identify which cell is behind and either reassign labor or adjust the schedule.
- Timeline: Must be resolved within one heartbeat (90 minutes) or the monument will starve.

Condition 2: Output Buffer At MAX Line (Flooding)

- Water Strider Action: Stop collecting work from Cell OUT squares. Notify the Supervisor.
- Supervisor Action: Identify why cells are overproducing. Likely cause: a cell is "building ahead" to look busy.
- Timeline: Cells must stop releasing until the buffer drains to Green.

Condition 3: Rejected Batch (Quality Gate Failure)

- Water Strider Action: Return the batch to the Cell OUT square with the Handoff Card marked "REJECTED" and the reason noted.
- Cell Operator Action: Fix the issue and resubmit on the next route.
- Tracking: Log every rejection on the Monument Scorecard. If rejections exceed 10% of batches in a week, conduct a root cause analysis with the cell team.

Condition 4: Monument Down

- Water Strider Action: Stop collecting new work. Place a Red Cone at every Cell OUT square. Notify cells to switch to alternative work (5S, maintenance, training, etc.).
- Monument Operator Action: Follow the Downtime Playbook (Chapter 6, Layer 3).
- Water Strider Resume: When the monument restarts, the Water Strider prioritizes draining the existing buffer before collecting new work.

Selecting the Right Person

The Water Strider is not your least experienced material handler. They are not the new hire you are trying to keep busy. This role requires a specific personality.

What to look for:

- **Comfortable saying no.** They will reject work from senior operators. They need the backbone to hold the line.
- **Consistent, not heroic.** You do not want the fastest forklift driver. You want the

person who runs the same route, at the same pace, every single time. Boring is beautiful.

- **Detail-oriented.** They are checking paperwork on every batch. If they skip the checklist, bad work enters the system.
- **Respected on the floor.** Cell operators must trust that the Water Strider is not playing favorites. The role works because it is impartial.

Training the Water Strider

Week 1: Shadow and Learn

- The Water Strider walks the route with the Supervisor. They learn every cell's OUT and IN squares, every Handoff Card field, and the Buffer Warning Line and Red Line locations.
- They do not make decisions. They observe.

Week 2: Supervised Execution

- The Water Strider runs the route independently. The Supervisor audits two routes per day, checking for correct Handoff

Card inspection and proper buffer level reporting.

- Common Week 2 problems: skipping the checklist under pressure, accepting verbal promises ("the paperwork is coming"), and deviating from the route to help with unrelated tasks.

Week 3: Independent with Audit

- The Water Strider runs independently. The Supervisor audits one route per day.
- By the end of Week 3, the Water Strider should be able to answer: "What is the buffer level right now?" within 5 seconds without looking.

Week 4: Certified

- The Supervisor conducts a final audit covering route timing, checklist compliance, escalation protocol, and Scorecard updates.
- The Water Strider is formally certified and recognized (name on the board, announcement at the team meeting).

The Backup Plan

The Water Strider takes vacations. The Water Strider gets sick. If you have no backup, the system dies on Day 1 of their absence.

Train a minimum of two backups. These are typically cell operators who rotate into the role one day per week to stay current. They must complete the same certification process.

Post the backup schedule visibly. Everyone on the floor should know: "If Maria is out, James runs the route."

The Small-Shop Question

In smaller shops, the Water Strider may be a part-time role tied to the heartbeat instead of a dedicated headcount. That is acceptable at launch. A cell lead or existing material handler can own the route during the constraint's peak windows.

What is not acceptable is shared ownership. One person must own feeding the monument, rejecting incomplete work, and closing the loop on returns during each shift. The role matters more than the title. What fails is not the lack of a job description — it is the lack of a single owner.

Common Mistakes

1. **Loading the Water Strider with other duties.** "While you're out there, can you also deliver supplies to the tool crib?" No. The route is sacred. Additional tasks cause delays, which cause starvation, which causes expediting. Every "small favor" costs you flow.

2. **Undermining the Gatekeeper authority.** A supervisor says, "Just take it, we'll fix the paperwork later." The moment this happens, every operator learns that the checklist is optional. The Plant Manager must publicly back the Water Strider's authority to reject work.

3. **No backup trained.** The Water Strider calls in sick on Monday. By Tuesday afternoon, there are 15 carts jammed around the oven and three cell leads screaming at each other. This is preventable.

4. **Skipping the Scorecard update.** The Buffer Health check at Stop 9 takes 2 minutes. Skipping it means leadership has

no visibility into system health. If the data stops, the support stops.

Implementation Checklist

- [ ] **Handoff Cards** printed and laminated.
- [ ] **Warning Line** marked at 50% of buffer.
- [ ] **Red Line** marked at the 25% of buffer
- [ ] **Tickets** created and distributed to cells.
- [ ] **Downtime Playbook** posted at the control panel.

Chapter 7

Measuring Success and Sustaining Results

You have identified the constraint, optimized the layout, and installed the material flow system. Now you must answer the question leadership will ask: **"Did it work?"**

Without measurement, you have opinions. With measurement, you have proof.

The Six Key Metrics (The Monument Scorecard)

Do not drown in data. Track these six metrics weekly to monitor the health of your shared resource.

1. Effective Utilization

- **Definition:** Percentage of time the monument is producing *good, scheduled parts.*
- **The Trap:** Do not confuse "Busy" with "Effective." Running unauthorized work to look busy is waste.
- **Target:** 70–85%.
- **The Highway Analogy:** A highway running at 100% utilization is a parking lot. Traffic (flow) moves fastest at 70–80% density. Your constraint is the same. You need that 20% gap for variability and changeovers.

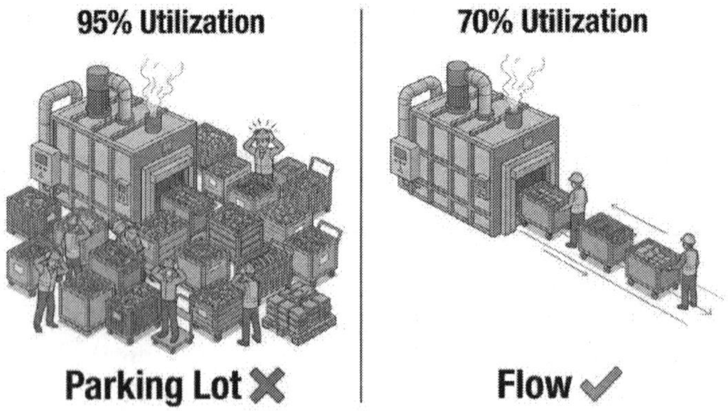

2. Changeover Trend

- **Definition:** The average time from "Last Good Piece" to "First Good Piece."
- **The Trap:** Averages hide problems. Track the **"Last 10 Average"** to see drift immediately.
- **Target:** Within 10% of your SMED standard.

3. Buffer Health

- **Definition:** Percentage of time the Input Buffer is in the "Green Zone."
- **The Trap:** If the buffer is always full, you have too much inventory. If it is always empty, you are starving the bottleneck.
- **Target:** >80% Green.

4. Constraint Lead Time

- **Definition:** The total time from *Release* (Cell OUT) to *Return* (Cell IN).
- **The Trap:** This is your truth serum. If utilization is high but lead time is growing, you are releasing work faster than the machine can run.

- **Target:** < 2x the Process Time.

5. Expedite Rate

- **Definition:** Percentage of jobs requiring a Priority Tag.
- **The Trap:** If everything is urgent, nothing is urgent.
- **Target:** < 20%.

6. Customer Service Level

- **Definition:** On-time delivery for the product families that use this monument.
- **Target:** Month-over-month improvement.

*See **Appendix A** for the **Monument Scorecard Template**.*

Calculating ROI: Hard vs. Soft Savings

To get budget for future improvements (or that second machine), you must speak the language of Finance. You must separate **Hard Savings** from **Soft Savings**.

Hard Savings (Cash in the Bank)

These are expenses you *stop paying*.

1. **Premium Freight:** Expedited shipping fees eliminated.
2. **Overtime:** Weekend shifts canceled because the monument runs efficiently during the week.
3. **Inventory Carrying Cost:** Cash released by lowering the WIP in the input and output buffers.
4. **Scrap:** Reduction in quality defects from rushing.

Soft Savings (Capacity Created)

This is potential revenue.

1. **Throughput Increase:** "We can now make 20% more valves per week."
2. **Labor Efficiency:** "Operators spend 10 hours less per week walking to the oven."

The Warning: Never mix these two numbers when presenting to the CFO.

- **Correct:** "We saved $80,000 in overtime (Hard) and created $1.2M in capacity potential (Soft)."
- **Incorrect:** "We saved $1.28M." (The CFO will reject this immediately because the bank account didn't go up by $1.2M).

*See **Appendix A** for the **Cost of Constraint ROI Worksheet**.*

The 60-Day Implementation Roadmap

Do not try to do everything on Monday. Use this phased approach.

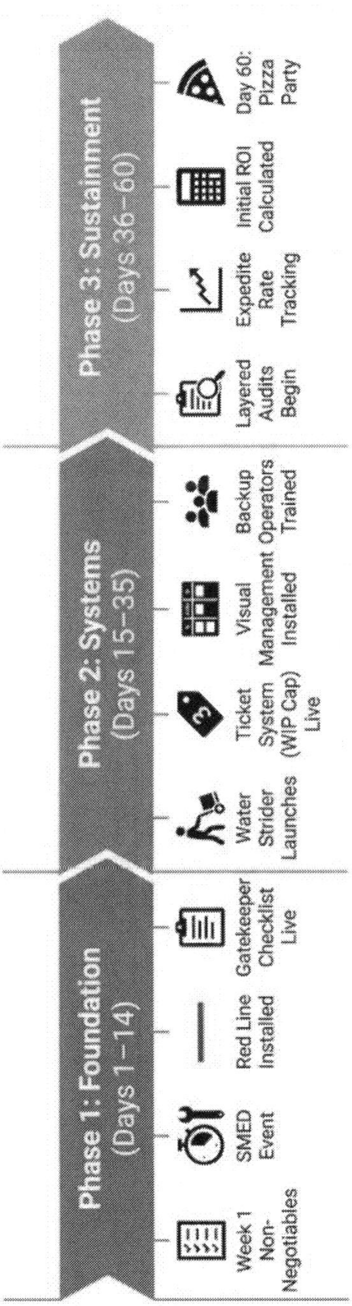
Phase 1: Foundation
(Days 1–14)
Week 1 Non-Negotiables
SMED Event
Red Line Installed
Gatekeeper Checklist Live
Phase 2: Systems
(Days 15–35)
Water Strider Launches
Ticket System (WIP Cap) Live
Visual Management Installed
Backup Operators Trained
Phase 3: Sustainment
(Days 36–60)
Layered Audits Begin
Expedite Rate Tracking
Initial ROI Calculated
Day 60: Pizza Party

Phase 1: Foundation (Days 1–14)

- **Focus:** Stability and Rules.
- **Key Actions:**
    - Announce the "Week 1 Non-Negotiables."
    - Execute the SMED event.
    - Install the "Warning and Red Lines" in the buffer.
    - Implement the Gatekeeper Checklist.

Phase 2: Systems (Days 15–35)

- **Focus:** Flow and Rhythm.
- **Key Actions:**
    - Launch the Water Strider route.
    - Implement the Ticket System (WIP Cap).
    - Install visual management (Heartbeat Timer, Andon Lights, etc.).
    - Train backups for the Monument Operator.

Phase 3: Sustainment (Days 36–60)

- **Focus:** Audit and Refine.
- **Key Actions:**
    - Begin Layered Audits (Daily/Weekly/Monthly).
    - Track the "Expedite Rate" and force it down.
    - Calculate initial ROI.
    - **Day 60:** Pizza Party (The Celebration Rule). Note that for some reason the pizza party has become quite the meme these days for employees who don't feel valued. So choose your celebration wisely.

The Celebration Rule

When you hit Day 60, **buy pizza**. Specifically, buy it for the **Water Strider** and the **Monument Operator**.

They bore the brunt of this change. They are the ones enforcing the rules when people yell at them. Publicly recognizing them cements the culture that "Process Discipline Matters."

Failure Modes: How to Prevent Backsliding

After working with hundreds of plants, we know exactly how this system fails. Watch for these three signals:

Failure Mode 1: SMED Regression

- **Signal:** Changeover times slowly creep up (e.g., 20 mins → 25 → 35).
- **Cause:** Operators stop doing external prep while the machine is running.
- **Fix:** Re-audit the "Pre-Flight Checklist." Tools must be staged *before* the machine stops.

Failure Mode 2: The "Just This Once" Override

- **Signal:** A supervisor orders the Water Strider to accept an incomplete kit because "it's hot."
- **Cause:** Lack of management discipline.
- **Fix:** If you break the gatekeeper rule once, the gate is broken forever. Plant Manager must step in and back the Water Strider.

Failure Mode 3: The Wallpaper Effect

- **Signal:** The Monument Scorecard is not updated for two weeks.
- **Cause:** No one looks at it, so the team stopped updating it.
- **Fix:** Force the weekly review meeting. Stand at the board. Use the data to make a decision.

The Gemba Test

How do you know if your system is real? Go to the monument. Stand there for 30 minutes. Ask yourself one question:

"Does the floor match the board?"

- If the board says "Green" but the operator is running around looking for a wrench... **Fail.**
- If the buffer says "4 hours" but there are 20 carts jammed in the aisle... **Fail.**
- If the schedule says "Product A" and the machine is running "Product B"... **Fail.**

If the floor matches the data, you have won. You have tamed the monster.

Final Thoughts

You have moved from "managing chaos" to "managing constraints."

- You stopped buying equipment you didn't need.
- You stopped scheduling by shouting.
- You empowered a Water Strider to protect your most valuable asset.

The constraint is sacred. Protect it, feed it, and it will feed your business.

Now, go to the Appendix and print your Toolkit.

Part 2

The Toolkit

Appendix A

Implementation Templates

Note to Reader: These templates are designed to be copied, printed, and laminated. Do not overcomplicate them with software. Start with paper.

Tool 1: The Monument Scorecard

Purpose: Weekly tracking of shared equipment performance.

Frequency: Reviewed every Monday morning.

[TEMPLATE START]

MONUMENT SCORECARD

Equipment: ______________________

Week Of: ______________________

Reviewed By: ______________________

1. Effective Utilization (% of time running paid work) Target: 70–85% This Week: ___________ Status: ☐ GREEN ☐ RED

2. Changeover Trend (Last 10 rolling average) Target: < 30 min This Week: ___________ Status: ☐ GREEN ☐ RED

3. Buffer Health (% of checks in Green Zone) Target: > 80% This Week: ___________ Status: ☐ GREEN ☐ RED

4. Constraint Lead Time (Release to Return) Target: < 2× Process Time This Week: ___________ Status: ☐ GREEN ☐ RED

5. Expedite Rate (% of jobs with Priority Tags) Target: < 20% This Week: ___________ Status: ☐ GREEN ☐ RED

Weekly Action Plan

Top Issue This Week:

____

Root Cause:

____

Action:

____

Owner: ____________Due Date: ____________

[TEMPLATE END]

Note: Track daily data on a printed, laminated version posted at the monument. Use this weekly summary for the Monday morning review. For a filled-in example showing daily tracking, see the Monument Scorecard example in this appendix.

Note: The Constraint Lead Time target should be set at less than 2× your actual process time. For example, if your heat treat cycle is 90 minutes, target less than 3–4 hours from Cell OUT to Cell IN.

Filled in Template Example

SHARED MACHINE SCORECARD - WEEK OF [DATE]

Metric	Target	Mon	Tue	Wed	Thu	Fri	Weekly Avg	Status
Effective Utilization	70-85%	74%	71%	78%	76%	73%	74%	GREEN
Changeover Trend	<30 min	22 min	24 min	21 min	28 min	23 min	24 min	GREEN
Buffer Health	>80% Green	85%	90%	75%	80%	88%	84%	YELLOW
Constraint Lead Time	<4 hrs	3.2 hrs	3.5 hrs	3.8 hrs	3.4 hrs	3.1 hrs	3.4 hrs	GREEN
Expedite Rate	<20%	18%	15%	22%	12%	10%	15%	GREEN

Weekly Action Plan
Top Issue: Buffer dipped Wednesday.
Root Cause: Cell B operator absent.
Action: Cross-train backup.
Owner: Sarah.
Due: Next Friday.

Tool 2: The Gatekeeper Checklist

Purpose: To prevent "phantom inventory" from entering the buffer.

User: Water Strider (or whoever moves work to the monument).

Rule: If *any* box is unchecked, the work stays in the cell.

[TEMPLATE START]

MONUMENT RELEASE CHECKLIST

Stop! Do not move work unless:

1. [ ] **Quantity Verified:** All parts present. No partial kits.
2. [ ] **Upstream Complete:** All previous operations signed off.
3. [ ] **Paperwork Attached:** Traveler, Drawing, and Recipe specified.
4. [ ] **Quality Check:** Parts are clean and defect-free.

5. [ ] **Container Correct:** Proper bin/basket/rack for the machine.
6. [ ] **Identification:** "OUT" Tag or Handoff Card attached.
7. [ ] **Buffer Space:** The Input Buffer has room for this batch.

Gatekeeper Signature: ________________

[TEMPLATE END]

Tool 3: The Monument Handoff Card

Purpose: Maintains chain of custody between Cell, Water Strider, and Monument. Attach this physical card to the batch.

[TEMPLATE START]

MONUMENT HANDOFF CARD

SECTION A: RELEASE (Filled by Cell Operator)

- **Cell:** ________ **Family:** ________ **Part #:** ________

- **Qty:** ________ **Recipe Code:** _______
- **Priority:** ☐ Standard ☐ Rush (Yellow) ☐ Emergency (Red)
- *I certify this batch is complete and ready.*
- **Signed (Cell Op):** ________________ **Time:** ________

SECTION B: RECEIPT (Filled by Monument Op)

- **Input Buffer Level at arrival:** ☐ Green ☐ Yellow ☐ Red
- *I verify the recipe matches the load.*
- **Signed (Monument Op):** __________ **Time:** ________

SECTION C: RETURN (Filled by Water Strider)

- **Process Complete.** Parts Cooled/Dried.
- **Returned to Cell IN Square.**
- **Signed (Water Strider):** ___________ **Time:** ________
- **Total Lead Time:** _______ Hours

[TEMPLATE END]

Tool 4: Cost of Constraint ROI Worksheet

Purpose: To justify investment in SMED, tooling, or duplicate equipment.

[TEMPLATE START]

COST OF CONSTRAINT CALCULATOR

PART 1: HARD COSTS (Cash we stop spending)

1. **Overtime:** (Annual OT hours at monument) x (OT Rate) = $___________
2. **Premium Freight:** (Annual expedited shipping fees) = $___________
3. **Scrap/Rework:** (Cost of quality errors at monument) = $___________
4. **Inventory:** (Value of WIP in input and output buffers x 20% carrying cost) = $___________

- **TOTAL HARD SAVINGS:** $___________ (A)

PART 2: SOFT COSTS (Capacity we gain)

5. **Lost Sales:** (Orders declined due to lead time) = $___________

6. **Throughput:** (Value of 20% capacity increase) = $___________

- **TOTAL SOFT SAVINGS:** $________ (B)

PART 3: INVESTMENT

7. **Equipment/Tooling Cost:** $___________

8. **Implementation Labor:** $___________

- **TOTAL INVESTMENT:** $_________ (C)

ROI CALCULATION

- **Payback Period:** (C) ÷ (A) = ___________ Months

(Note: Use Hard Savings only for conservative payback)

[TEMPLATE END]

Tool 5: Water Strider Standard Work Template

[TEMPLATE START]

WATER STRIDER STANDARD WORK

Equipment Served: ________________________
Route Frequency: Every ________ minutes (= half the Heartbeat) Shift: ________________________

ROUTE STOPS:

Stop	Location	Action	Target Time
1	Monument OUT	Pick up finished work. Collect Tickets.	______ min
2	Cell ____ IN	Deliver finished parts. Return Ticket.	______ min
3	Cell ____ OUT	Inspect Handoff Card. Load if ready.	______ min

Stop	Location	Action	Target Time
4	Cell ____ IN	Deliver finished parts. Return Ticket.	______ min
5	Cell ____ OUT	Inspect Handoff Card. Load if ready.	______ min
6	Cell ____ IN	Deliver finished parts. Return Ticket.	______ min
7	Cell ____ OUT	Inspect Handoff Card. Load if ready.	______ min
8	Monument IN	Deliver new work. Check buffer vs. Warning Line / Red Line.	______ min
9	Scorecard	Update Buffer Health (Green / Yellow / Red).	______ min

Total Route Target: ________minutes

Slack Time: _______ minutes (Do NOT fill with other tasks)

ESCALATION TRIGGERS:

Condition	**Action**	**Notify**
Buffer below Warning Line	Watch, check upstream	N/A
Buffer below Red Line	Escalate. Red Cone at monument.	Supervisor immediately
Buffer above MAX	Stop collecting from cells.	Supervisor within 15 min
Rejected batch	Return to cell. Mark card "REJECTED."	Log on Scorecard
Monument down	Red Cone at all Cell OUT squares.	Supervisor + all Cell Leads

GATEKEEPER CHECKLIST

(Applied at every Cell OUT stop):

□ Quantity verified (no partial kits)

□ Upstream operations complete

□ Traveler and recipe attached

□ Handoff Card signed by Cell Operator

□ Ticket attached

□ Container correct for monument

If ANY box is unchecked: REJECT. Work stays in the cell.

Water Strider Name: ________________________
Backup 1: ________________________

Backup 2: ________________________

Certified Date: ________________________

[TEMPLATE END]

Appendix B

Case Study: Precision Components Inc.

Throughout the book, we referenced Precision Components Inc. Here is their full story, consolidated from chaos to control. Note that the names and data have been changed. The situation remains as a teaching point and example.

The Situation

Precision Components manufactures hydraulic valve bodies. They have three machining cells (Cell A, B, and C) producing 45 different product families.

The Constraint: All three cells feed into one centralized **Heat Treat Oven**.

- **The Symptom:** Lead time through the shop was 4 weeks. Lead time through the oven alone was 5 days.
- **The Behavior:** Cell leads fought over oven time. Expedite meetings happened daily at 8:00 AM. 35% of all jobs had "Red Priority Tags."
- **The Cost:** They were spending $85,000/year on overtime and losing $180,000/year in sales due to long lead times.

Phase 1: The Diagnosis (Chapters 1 & 2)

The Plant Manager, Sarah, wanted to buy a second oven ($250,000). Before signing the check, they ran the **Constraint Type Test**.

- **Utilization:** The oven was running 72% of the time.
- **Changeovers:** Averaged 93 minutes.
- **Conclusion:** This was not a *Capacity* problem (yet). It was a *Scheduling* problem. The oven sat idle for hours while operators

searched for baskets, then ran massive batches to avoid the 93-minute setup penalty.

Decision: "Earn the right to buy." Fix the flow first.

Phase 2: The Foundation (Chapters 3 & 4)

Sarah implemented the **Week 1 Non-Negotiables**:

1. **Release Rules:** Cells were forbidden from dumping parts at the oven unless the kit was 100% complete.
2. **SMED:** The team video-recorded a changeover. They found 40 minutes were spent looking for fixtures. They installed a **Shadow Board** and pre-staged loads.
    - *Result:* Changeover dropped from 93 mins → 24 mins.
3. **Layout:** They painted **Yellow Squares** (OUT) and **Green Squares** (IN) at each cell and at the oven. No parts were allowed on the floor outside these squares.

Phase 3: The System (Chapters 5 & 6)

With setup time reduced, they didn't need to run massive batches. They implemented a **Hybrid Strategy**:

1. **Time-Slicing:** Cell A got the oven from 6am–10am. Cell B from 10am–2pm. Cell C from 2pm–6pm.
2. **The Water Strider:** They assigned John (a material handler) to run a fixed route every 45 minutes. John became the **Gatekeeper**, rejecting any cart without a signed Handoff Card.
3. **Visual Management:** They painted a **Red Line** at the 25% mark in the oven input buffer.
    - *Above the line:* Green (Keep running).
    - *Below the line:* Red (Crisis – Call Supervisor).

The Result (Chapter 7)

After 60 days, the transformation was validated by Finance:

- **Changeover:** Sustained at 24 minutes.
- **Lead Time:** Dropped from 5 days → 1.5 days.
- **Expedites:** Dropped from 35% → 12%.
- **Financials:** They saved the $250k capital expense (didn't buy the oven) and eliminated $45k in overtime.

The Lesson: The oven wasn't the bottleneck. The lack of a system was the bottleneck. By managing the constraint, they unlocked the capacity of the entire factory.

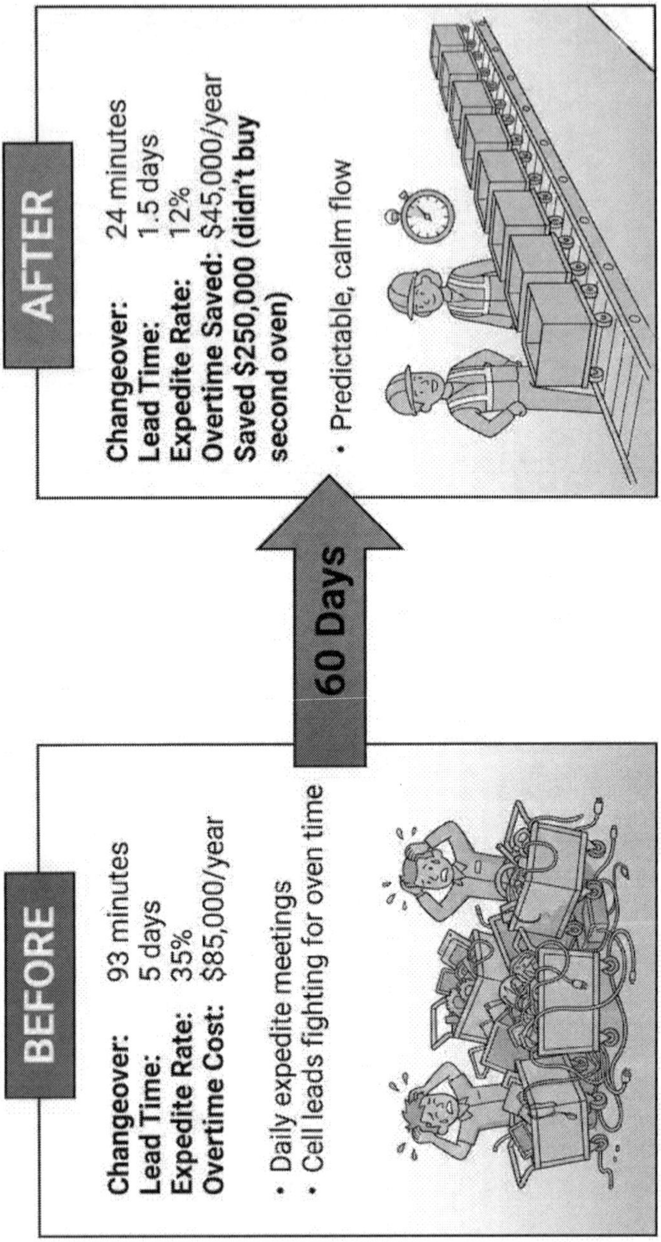
BEFORE
Changeover: 93 minutes
Lead Time: 5 days
Expedite Rate: 35%
Overtime Cost: $85,000/year
• Daily expedite meetings
• Cell leads fighting for oven time
60 Days
AFTER
Changeover: 24 minutes
Lead Time: 1.5 days
Expedite Rate: 12%
Overtime Saved: $45,000/year
Saved $250,000 (didn't buy second oven)
• Predictable, calm flow

What's Next: The Second Half of the Constraint Problem

The strategies in this book solve the **access problem**.

They help you stop the daily fights over the schedule, establish clear routing rules, protect the constraint, and stabilize shared equipment that multiple cells or value streams depend on.

But some shared resources create a second problem.

They do not just require scheduling. They also require **batching**.

A large CNC, CMM, or specialized inspection station may process one part at a time. In that case, the main challenge is access: who gets the resource, when they get it, and how the queue is controlled.

But machines like heat treat ovens, industrial washers, paint booths, plating tanks, curing ovens, autoclaves, and test chambers often require multiple parts to run at once. Even with perfect scheduling, these machines can still force parts to accumulate before the process and release work in large bursts afterward.

That is a different problem.

Shared equipment is an access and scheduling problem.
Batch processing is a flow disruption problem.

Some machines are only shared resources.
Some machines are only batch processors.
Some machines are both.

Volume 7 taught you how to control access to shared equipment.

Volume 8, **Designing Flow Around Batch Processors for High-Mix, Low-Volume Manufacturing**, teaches you how to protect flow when a process refuses to run one piece at a time.

In that direct companion guide, you will learn how to isolate the batching, separate process batches from transfer batches, calculate input and output buffers, design timed release cycles, and protect upstream and downstream flow without pretending every batch processor can magically disappear.

If your constraint is both shared and batched, use this book to control access, then use Volume 8 to control the batching.

About the Author

Nick Arkesteyn is a manufacturing expert with over 20 years of Lean Manufacturing experience. Rising through the ranks from R&D and Quality Engineer to Production Manager and Director of Operations, Nick has seen the chaos from many angles—from the drawing board to the shipping dock.

He is the founder of **Lean Line Pro**, a consultancy dedicated to helping manufacturers organize complexity and improve flow. His mission is simple: to prove that even the most complex high-mix operations can achieve world-class flow.

To learn more or access free training tools, visit: **www.LeanLinePro.com**

Books In This Series

Lean Line Pro Deep Dive Series is a step-by-step implementation series for building real lean flow in high-mix, low-volume manufacturing.

Each volume is designed around one outcome: one completed improvement project. No academic lean theory. No fluff. Just practical methods, templates, and tools you can use immediately on the shop floor.

Start at Volume 1 and build a complete production system—one layer at a time.

Book 1: Product Families for High-Mix, Low-Volume Manufacturing

The foundation of HMLV lean. Learn how to group hundreds or thousands of parts into families based on shared routings, then use those families to unlock everything that follows.

Book 2: SMED Quick Changeover for High-Mix, Low-Volume Manufacturing

Slash your changeover times from hours to minutes. When changeovers are fast, small batches become economically viable, and everything downstream gets easier.

Book 3: Flexible Cell Design for High-Mix, Low-Volume Manufacturing

Design a production cell that can flex across dozens of products without chaos. This book shows how to build work cells that flow, balance labor, reduce travel, and prevent bottlenecks.

Book 4: Mixed-Model Scheduling (Heijunka) for High-Mix, Low-Volume Manufacturing

Build a leveled schedule for your flexible cell. Learn heijunka, EPE calculations, and daily scheduling rhythms that work in real shops.

Book 5: Material Flow & Pull Systems for High-Mix, Low-Volume Manufacturing

Install the kanban, supermarkets, FIFO lanes, water strider routes, and pull discipline that keep materials flowing. The circulatory system your lean line needs to actually work.

Book 6: Standard Work for High-Mix, Low-Volume Manufacturing

Traditional standard work fails in high-mix environments because it tries to document every product instead of the process. This book shows you how to standardize the 80% that's consistent while handling the 20% that varies—using setup sheets, matrices, and reference systems that actually get followed. Includes templates for process documentation, inspection standards, training matrices, and sustainment systems.

Book 7: Shared Equipment Management for High-Mix, Low-Volume Manufacturing

For when two or more cells in your plant share one machine. Maybe it's a heat treat oven, a paint booth, a plating line, or a CNC machining center.

You cannot duplicate it. You cannot eliminate it. And the daily scheduling fights are killing your flow. This book teaches the six strategies for managing shared equipment, including Campaign Wheels, the Water Strider role, and the Ticket System, so you can stop scheduling by shouting and start running your constraint with boring, predictable consistency..

Book 8: Designing Flow Around Batch Processors for High-Mix, Low-Volume Manufacturing

This book is for when you have a station or operation in your cell that needs to run a batch process and you want to preserve your single-piece-flow.

Inside, you'll get five practical, zero-capital strategies to isolate the batching, protect downstream flow, and keep your line moving. You'll learn how to use decoupling buffers, timed release cycles, and master the process-vs-transfer batch distinction.

A Note from the Author

If you found this book helpful, there are two great ways you can help support others in the industry and a third option if your own team needs a little support.

1. Leave a Quick Review

Please take a moment to leave a review on the site where you purchased this book. Honest reviews are the single best way to help other operations leaders discover these methods and start taming the chaos in their own shops.

2. Help Improve the System

Continuous improvement applies to books too.

If you apply this system, I would love to hear what happened. Send me your success stories, lessons learned, before-and-after results, questions, or improvement ideas.

If you measure the system and find a gap, I want to know about it. If you identify an issue or missing piece in any of these books that leads to a future update, I will send you the revised PDF edition completely free of charge.

(This is exactly why there is a revised and expanded edition of Volume 3 — a reader found a gap, and a major update followed.)

Please send any feedback, questions, or improvement ideas directly through LeanLinePro.com/contact.

3. Need Help Implementing?

Reading about continuous improvement is the easy part. The real challenge is making it work on your actual shop floor, especially when the daily fires are burning and the schedule is constantly shifting. You don't have to figure out the implementation alone.

For teams that have the hands to do the work but need expert direction to get there faster, I offer structured Remote Coaching. We will assess your current situation and work through the implementation together.

Link: https://calendly.com/nickarkesteyn/30min

Thank you,

Nick Arkesteyn

Made in the USA
Monee, IL
05 November 2026

67843129R00106